STRUGGLE FOR EXISTENCE

Mamata Banerjee

STRUGGLE FOR EXISTENCE

MAMATA BANERJEE

MAGVISUAL PRIYONKAR PUBLICATIONS

IN ARRANGEMENT WITH

COSMO PUBLICATIONS

NEW DELHI 1998

First Published 1998

ISBN 81-7020-829-7

STRUGGLE FOR EXISTENCE
MAMATA BANERJEE

Published by :
MAGVISUAL PRIYONKAR PUBLICATIONS
23,N.S.Road,
Calcutta - 700001.
IN ARRANGEMENT WITH

MRS. RANI KAPOOR
for COSMO PUBLICATIONS Div. of
GENESIS PUBLISHING PVT. LTD.
24-B, Ansari Road,
Darya Ganj,
New Delhi-110002, INDIA

Typeset at :
Crest Graphics,Calcutta

Printed at :
Mehra Offset Press

Dedicated to the memory of the greatest martyr of free India, the never-ending flame in the dark world of politics

RAJIV GANDHI

Explanations

My induction in politics was at a very early age. Gradually twenty seven years have passed by in the arena of politics. The infallibility of a strong conscience has at times broadened the path to truthful confessions. Sometimes, I put myself to trial at the door of my conscience and analyse myself. Then the stark reality of certain incidents are freed from the depth of the mind-these are my very own true thoughts.

It is not that I have not faced failure during the course of my life. Many a dream has been shattered by a succession of blows. However, these experiences have helped me to gain a more clear insight-I have been able to see through the present day domain of life and deteriorating values in politics that shield the truth-it is all a game of dice.

While narrating the incidents, both factual and true (sometimes unpalatable), I may have written much about myself, but this is not an autobiography. For the time being, my writing is confined to the submission of certain facts based upon what I have truly perceived.

I am not a writer, so there may exist certain faults in the style of narration for which I seek forgiveness. It has not been my intention to hurt anyone personally, nor cast any insinuations. My aim is to place before the people's court, my personal conception of things so that the ideals and values of politics may give a clue to the new generation about the path to be followed amidst today's stark reality. I hope it will enrich their future.

The inspiration behind this book comes from the blessings and warm wishes that I have received from the countless people. In fact, the roots of my "Grassroots" politics lie in them. I offer my sincerest respect and love to them. It is a great opportunity for me to pay my respect to the former Prime Minister of India, Rajiv Gandhi, the never-ending flame which showed me the path in the dark world of politics. I also pay homage to the immortal martyrs of 21st July—they who sang the victory song while laying down their lives on the wide thoroughfares of Calcutta.

Mamata Banerjee

January, 1998

1

PART

There is no doubt that self-analysis is necessary in everyone's life. During life's journey one faces many cross-roads and it is self-introspection of the past, the blows and counter-blows that one experiences which help in making decisions for the future. That is why, after nearly half my life is over, I am looking back a trip down memory lane.

I do not hesitate in acknowledging that after travelling the difficult passage of life, sometimes the formidable path, I have reached a point where I am tallying the pros and cons of life's experiences, pondering over the errors in judgement that I have made, the pain I have felt in not being able to do many things that I have longed to do. Nevertheless, a sense of pride prevails; inspite of the minor mistakes, the people's endless affection has purified me, overwhelmed me. Their trust in me has enthused me, and been the basic driving force. I am grateful to those who have stood by me, both during my days of sorrow and joy, trouble and danger, with their sincere co-operation and whole-hearted support. I am grateful to those who have constantly opposed me, in every step that I have taken, have struck blow after blow at me. From this I got the opportunity to think afresh, and amidst stark reality to really get to know the ways of the world.

Many critics say that I am strongly influenced by my emotions-that, this is my life's biggest folly. I fully agree with the critics. In my life's course, in the series of events, in every milestone, a touch of my conscience is evident. The source of emotion is conceived from the heart, is perceived from the depths of the soul. The perception that is the source of all creation, the feeling that constantly awakens in man the realisation to do something for the welfare of mankind, country, society-that is emotion. Emotions can neither be bought, nor created by force. Unless a person sincerely feels for others and their sorrow, sadness and want do not penetrate him, then, however powerful he may be in the spheres of economics or politics, emotion does not exist in him.

Netaji Subhash Chandra Bose has also, (in "Youth's Dream") mentioned emotion and feeling, sacrifice and perceptions. By being emotional, sometimes mistakes can happen, at times things may go right, some may lose, and some may be displaced. However, it is emotion of the soul which brings light to the conscience. It strikes upon the conscience and gives the strength to tread the path which is pure and truthful.

In my childhood I never thought that I would enter such a large arena of politics, become an M.P., find a place in the Union Cabinet or organise a historic public meeting at Calcutta's Brigade Parade grounds with the blessings and affection of the people. Perhaps it is a political vortex which has directed me to this place-I condemn and dislike politics based upon counterfeit emotions. Such emotions clash with idealism.

My late father planted the seeds of idealism within me and taught me about the values of humanitarianism. This still inspires me. I think "they who have only given and not received-they who are deprived-they who are oppressed-those whose tears are not taken notice of-they who never understood why in their sorrowful existence they have no rights-it is the sorrow of such persons which has made me speak up and place before the people their grievances." These words of Sarat Chandra Chattopadhyay are a major source of strength in our struggle.

When I realise that this is a different age, where idealism is not valued, truth has no worth, sacrifice has no reward, value-based politics is non-existent-only narrow, confined party-lines exist, self-interest is the distinctive quality, leading lives of wanton indulgence, speaking lies, shedding crocodile tears for the people is the practice, then I lie awake night after night. From afar, I hear the nocturnal bird's call. The deep darkness of the night intensifies. I look at my father's photograph and ask-why? Why did you encourage me to enter this dirty game of chess (politics)?

My conscience is stricken when I see many wrongs, but cannot protest in case this goes against us. Like the dreaded cobra's bite, the deep night asks me-have you still not learnt your lesson? Are you still dreaming of doing something worthwhile? You will fail, you will fail! The world is so ruthless and cruel. It is a haven for the seekers and has no place for the sacrificer. Misleading the people, unmoved by their sorrows! What is the necessity of stirring the hornet's nest? One will get stung-this is inevitable.

I do not know whether the dreams and hopes with which I entered politics will be ever fulfilled. Every individual has a specific goal and direction in life. I too had a dream-of doing something worthwhile with a humanitarian outlook. I have not given up. The hurt that is mine from shattered dreams does make my hands shake while I write this-but all is not over. Yes, I am worried when I see the web of intrigues in politics. I am alarmed because we do not fit into the scheme of things.

I was a bit different from others from childhood. When I was in Class IX, and my friends spoke of so many things, I would sit quietly in one corner, thinking. While in Class X, my friends talked about going to college, dressing-up and clothes. I would just gaze at them. I had never thought of what I would do after schooling was over. I carried with me the worried thoughts of my younger brothers and sister. My mother had been unwell-I would get up at 3.30 a.m., finish the entire cooking, get my brothers and sister ready for the day, and then, somehow, make it to school. Again, after school, I would rush back to cook the evening meal. When did I have the time to dream of the future?

Then came college-life, and with it the active participation in politics. My father had just died. Only God is a witness to the trauma of those days, and our struggle for existence. I still remember the day I entered active politics. The feeling of exultation, the intention to do endless work, the idealism. Early in the morning I would go to college. I have helped innumerable students with their studies and otherwise.

There was a D.S.O. union in our college. I started the Chhatra Parisad union. I was able to bring within my grip the protagonists of the Leftist union-movement in our college. Hence, within a very short time, a strong union like the D.S.O. failed to keep up with us.

I have received boundless affection from my teachers, the college staff and fellow-pupils. When I stayed away from class, to help with the admission of new students, my professors would not start the lessons without me and asked the other students to bring me back to class. I will not forget those college days of intense struggle (student movement). For that had been the toil and endeavour to nurture a seedling to a full bloomed plant.

From 1972 till 1977 West Bengal had a Congress Government. Many had offered me jobs. I did not take up any job because that would not have given me time for politics. In those days we were not in the habit of visiting any political leaders at their residences or taking any favours from them. Yet, I had taken up the fight with the D.S.O. at the college to such lengths that all the leaders were familiar with my name. In this way my college days passed by. In the year 1977, the general election took place and Smt. Indira Gandhi lost. Priyada (Priya Ranjan Das Munshi) also lost from the South Calcutta constituency. I had felt very sad, but at that time I did not fully understand the intrigues of politics on a larger sphere. I joined the University of Calcutta for my post-graduation studies. Then the CPI(M) was in power. I could not attend classes for one year. Next year I attended the classes and passed in the examinations. During that time there was a lot of public unrest concerning Smt. Indira Gandhi. We also joined the agitations. Indiraji was arrested. In Calcutta we were also arrested. I was then studying for B.Ed. course at Sree Shiksayatan College. In those days, any agitational programme ended up with arrests. With examinations scheduled for the next day I would be glancing through the text books inside the police lock-up and after getting released in the evening I would appear for the examinations the next morning. The next day there would be another agitational programme. Amidst this situation, I completed the Masters, B.Ed. and LLB degree course. I undertook training in work education also. Alongside my studies the protest movements continued-after all, wherever there is wrong there is protest.

During the Janata Party regime, Indiraji was harassed in many ways. She was being persecuted with a vengeance. After being elected as an M.P I came to know from Smt. Saroj Khapard (Rajya Sabha MP) how Indiraji was denied train reservation also. There were meetings, protests and marches everyday against the harassment meted out to Indiraji.

At that time, the then Prime Minister, Mr. Morarji Desai was arriving at Calcutta. We would have to show our protest. Subrata Mukherjee (Congress Party MLA) decided on a Black Flag demonstration. We were instructed to stand with black flags when the PM's motorcade would pass by. The police were keeping us under strict survelliance so that the PM's motorcade could pass without difficulty. I had told Pradipda not to worry about me-I would wave the black flag at Morarji Desai at the right moment.

The police was familiar with my name but not my appearence-this was to be my advantage. I stood in a corner like a very quiet girl so that nobody would suspect me. The slogans started as soon as the PM's motorcade appeared and I outwitted the police completely and raised the black flag right on the PM's limousine.

Many of us had to suffer torture after Indiraji's electoral defeat. Yet, I had not been afraid. I had bravely gone ahead with the protest programmes, I do not know what is the source of this strength! In our locality, the CPI(M) had pitted some muscle-men against me and my family. I have seen them torturing people openly and extorting money from the poor. If there was any protest, they would use the red-hot clothes-iron (taken from the small laundry beside my house) to scorch the body of the person who had protested. Which civilised individual can tolerate such things?

One day I strongly protested and said that such hooliganism would have to stop. In retaliation, they threw bombs at my house. My family members were accosted with daggers and swords when they went out on the road. All this was reported at the Police Station daily, but who would give justice? At that time the Congress Party was not in power at the Centre and the State. I organised a women's group at my neighbourhood and started a movement. The hoodlums, with the help of the party in power complained to the police that my family members and I were anti-socials. The police, on seeing us, expressed their surprise that such an allegation had been made about us. The police report was in our favour. The musclemen even tried to run me over with their car, but friends pushed me aside and my life was saved.

Now an incident happened. My elder brother (dada) was then newly married. His wife's name is Chandana. She is younger than me, a girl from the same neighbourhood. I was in the habit of calling her by her name. Dada and Chandana were walking down the road. The youngmen of the neighbourhood had all been invited for a feast and had gone there. So, taking advantage of the situation, the hoodlums attacked my dada. I was with my sister at home. Suddenly I saw a sobbing Chandana running towards us. I came to know of the attack on Dada. I and my sister immediately ran out. My sister has a weak heart because she had been ill quite often since her childhood. She does not resemble me and my brothers, but she has more courage than many others. She caught hold of the collar of one of the hoodlums and I delivered a few punches and rescued my dada. By then other persons of the neighbourhood had rushed over to us. Then it was a case of "escape and survive" for the "brave" hoodlums.

In this way we continued to tackle such situations and the hoodlum gang broke up into separate groups. some lost their lives in inter-group clashes. Some left the neighbourhood. Some tried to turn into new leaves and we helped them. Some were provided with jobs and they are now leading peaceful family lives. Actually, if anti-social people are treated with humaneness and sincerity, then they do change for the better. Nobody is an anti-social individual by birth. In truth, some power-wielding men make them anti-social persons and lead them into the wrong path.

Many incidents have followed, I remember the Students' Council elections at Ashutosh College. We were holding a meeting at the entrance of the college. In those days I could raise slogans for two hours at a stretch. My voice had become hoarse from raising slogans for two hours at a stretch at the meeting. Ashok, my colleague, said, "Didi, let us go and drink some water". As we reached the rear door of the college to go to the water tap, we saw that a well-known CPI(M) hoodlum was forcibly pushing my two colleagues of the Chhatra Parisad in a taxi (name-Anup and Moloy). This particular CPI(M) hoodlum has now quietened down. I knew about this person because I had heard about a murder in which he was implicated. What could we do! We were two in number (Ashoka and myself) whereas they totalled four. The two boys (Moloy and Anup) would possibly die without anybody knowing. So we did not wait for anybody and swung into action. I do not know how we did it, perhaps, God gave us the courage. I caught hold of the infamous hoodlum and before anybody realised what was happening, Ashoka started raining blows on him. They were not prepared for this and a lot of shouting ensued. Many people rushed to the spot within seconds. The policemen who had been at the front gate also came. The lives of the two boys were saved because of our timely action.

Now the CPI(M) attacked us with sten guns, bombs and pistol. They surrounded us. The situation at Hazra Road turned frightfully violent. Armed CPI(M) cadres were running after me. Do you know how I was saved that day? Many may have forgotton but I have not. There is a restaurant (Sangu Valley) next to the Sree Hari Mistanna Bhandar (a sweet-meats shop) opposite the Bhowanipur Police Station. A few young men were sitting inside the restaurant. Seeing the situation, they pulled me inside and closed the collapsible gate and door. My life was saved entirely because of their help. Otherwise, the CPI(M) would have killed me that very day.

Then started another chapter-political movements everyday, arrests everyday. Out of the 365 days in a year, I have been arrested on 330 days. Subratada announced that we would march to Writers' Buildings. We had all assembled for the march-my Women's Brigade was also there. The CPI(M) had just come to power. They too assembled as a countermove and then attacked us from all sides in pincer formation. They dragged many of my colleagues inside a government office building in Park Street and slashed them with razors. Everyone was injured and bleeding and trying to escape wherever they could. In this situation I saw many leaders fled from the scene-and the police force's job was to beat up the Party workers after making the leaders move away from the scene. Many of our women workers who had been injued were in agony. I saw one of our leaders fleeing by getting into a public transport bus. I had asked him why he was escaping? His answer was, each person should save his own skin. I saw another leader running away in the same fashion. When I asked him, he explained that he was leaving for Malda because he had an important meeting there. Now only a few of us were left standing on the road with the Party flag. The CPI(M) cadres ordered us to roll up the flag. We refused and told them that this was the tricolour and we would hold it higher. If they had the power, they could kill us but we would not move away.

I remember Mr. Ashok Sen was then the President of the State Unit of the Indian National Congress. There was to be a civil disobedience programme. A protest meeting was held at Esplanade. There boys died in the police firing. The police had turned violent and myself and about 100 colleagues were in their midst. At that point the police did not care for their own actions-they were beating up who-ever they could catch and throwing tear gas shells. We ran inside the Bhowanipur Club Tent. By then many were crying out of sheer fright. We were thinking that we would go out when the situation would quieten down. Outside, the place was a battlefield. Inside, we were discussing. At this juncture the police came inside the club tent. Initially, they started to beat up my brother Amit and Subrata Bakshi and started to drag them out. Their eyes blazed with the fire of revenge. If the police had succeeded in taking them out of the tent on that day, they would certainly have killed them both (Amit and Subrata Bakshi). We ladies surrounded the police and said, "Why are you catching us? We are just visitors here and we got caught in the melee. Can't you see that the number of boys and girls are the same?" The police accepted our explanations and we deceived the police by walking out in pairs. After seeing to it that everyone had gone out I left the tent. This then was life of politics-fear and apprehension at every step. Yet, this did not lower our enthusiasm-in fact it increased our enthusiasm.

Our agitation was at its peak. Suddenly, one afternoon,

we received the news of Indiraji's arrest. It was decided that a protest demonstration would be held in front of the old Doordarshan Kendra beside the Bangur Hospital at Tollygunge. Congress workers were very restless. While the meeting was in progress the road was blocked and the police charged with their batons. There followed the inevitable clash between the police and the Congress workers. After beating up Mr. Pankaj Banerjee the police became frenzied. We entered the Bangur Hospital compound. Then the hospital authorities closed down the main gate. On the other side, the agitation was at its height and the police were firing indiscriminately. Then, I alongwith other girls forcibly opened the gate for the passerbys and Congress workers, to save them from the firing. Outside, many congress workers stood with their backs to the wall to save themselves from the bullets. In those days, such incidents had happened repeatedly. Yet, there was no giving up, no fear. There was only the pledge to take up more agitational programmes. After this-what more?

Next day was the day of the general strike called by the Congress Party in West Bengal. Barkatda (Barkat Ghani Khan Chowdhury) was the President of the West Bengal unit of the Congress Party. Subratada (Subrata Mukherjee) was the General Secretary. On the day of the general strike, at about 8 a.m. I went to Subratada's residence with three women colleagues. He was asleep. I woke him up and reminded him that although a strike had been called, the traffic was moving about as usual. I told him, "Let us go and start a procession". Subratada said, ""You are four in number and with me, we are five. How can we start a procession?" I told him. "Come, we are with you". Then Subratada came out with us. The procession started at Gariahat and Subratada walked in front of us. I was right behind him and my three colleagues observed the Bandh in their own style-they were really mischievous! The procession which had started at Gariahat with five persons ended with about five hundred. Everything closed down. We escorted Subratada home and walked back to our residences. Within a short time came the news that Subratada had been arrested on charges of causing violence. It is true that from 1976 till 1983 it was under Subratada's leadership that agitational programmes were organised one after another. Jayantada, Ashokeda, Pradipda, Susobhanda, Bakshida, Bani, Aloke, Balu, Tama had all worked very hard and risked their lives. Yet, after that period the agitations changed course and hid its face inside the quicksand. If anyone becomes too active in Congress politics, then the top leadership draws him back with a strong hand. Perhaps, because of this Subratada was left out of the State Committee of the Congress. Stay indoors quietly and you are good, really good. Give lectures, send reports to the leadership, make money and share a portion of it-this has to be the "Political" agenda. This is reality.

Some leaders are victims of this reality. Whatever directives come from above are like the edict and must be obeyed. As if these are God's commands and nobody has the guts to disobey. Nowadays, I feel that Subratada's revolutionary spirit must have been dealt a blow in this way and removed him from the path of agitations. Many may criticise him for his present profile, but we realise the truth. Subratada has many a time made derogatory remarks about me. I have felt hurt but never retaliated with any remarks of this sort. That is because I feel that this is a reward in my political career. He who has the right can only criticise. Subratada taught us how to carry out political agitations and I am grateful to him. Many persons think that Subratada inducted me into politics, but this is not correct. I entered active politics in 1970. At that time the persons who had helped me most were Partha Roy Chowdhury (presently the President of South Calcutta District Congress Committee). Ranjit Ghosh, Ranada, (the then General Secretary of the Block Congress Committee) and Dilip Majumder (at present a Councillor of the Calcutta Municipal Corporation and a Borough Chairman).

In 1980 Indiraji returned to power. From 1983 I entered the larger arena of politics. In that year, the AICC session was held at Calcutta. Subratada was the Chairman of the Accomodation Sub-Committee, Subratada had taken up the entire responsibility because Pranabda (Pranab Mukherjee) had requested him. As we were in Subratada's team, he had left the entire responsibility of the VIPs' accommodation on us in good faith. Pranabda knew of my name, but we had never met each other. After seeing the work that was done, it was all praises. Rajiv Gandhi was then the General Secretary of AICC and Kamalapathi Tripathi was the Working President. I got the opportuniny to see Rajivji from close proximity. He used to go out at 6 a.m. and return at 1 a.m. Vincent George used to be with him all the time. Nobody had to put in any extra work for Rajivji, but the problem was with the aged leader Kamalapathi Tripathi. Subratada had told me "He will eat the food which has been cooked by a lady of the Brahmin caste only. For the morning, keep some juice of pistachios, cashew nuts and raisins".

I told my colleague Anima Chatterjee to take up the responsibility of cooking the food, but she said that she would require two helpers because she would not be able to manage on her own. I replied-"Wait, we will outwit the old gentleman. Two of my non-Brahmin colleagues (ladies) will do the cooking and you can serve the food. Then the job will be done without any problems for us". Everything went according to plan. Perhaps what we had done was wrong! Tripathiji is no more. If he was alive he would have fired me.

I have heard that unless one prostrated oneself at his feet, he would not look at the person. Tell me Reader, do these things suit today's world of science and logic? When I was young, my father had taught me that the true humaniterianism does not differentiate between caste and creed.

When I was young, I used to see my father return with the rickshaw laden with purchases. The children would come running with him (neighbourhood children). There used to be one bag for the family and the rest of the bags would contain mangoes, oranges or lozenges and biscuits. My father then used to point to the children and tell me to divide those amongst them and I used to do it gleefully. My father used to help people as far as possible-be it for anyone's daughter's marriage, children's school fees or household expenses. My mother used to tell him, "You are doing so much, but your own children are growing up. You don't think of them at all. Have you thought of what will happen to them?" In reply, my father used to tell her, "Just see, everything will be allright. God looks after those who have nobody to take care of them." I used to think that I would follow my father's ideals and stand by the have-nots.

As long as my father was alive, I did not know what want was. My father had a building materials business and used to earn a lot. He possessed land, a house and lorries. His most valuable asset however was his goodwill. The neighbours used to call him "Pandit Moshai" (learned person). He used to read the Gita (Hindu Scriptures) and pray everyday. He was a plain and simple man who had given his assets to friends in their hours of need.

The blow struck when father fell ill with gastric ulcers at the age of 41. He was a Government contractor and a lot of bills were due from the Government. He tried very hard to get the money so that his medical treatment could be arranged properly. At that time those friends for whom he had done so much turned their faces away. Father died (literally because of lack of medical treatment) at the PG Hospital on 9.2.72. It was fate. My elder brother was then only 17 years old and I was 15. The person who had helped others throughout his life could not get enough money for his own medical treatment. I and my family members will bear the burden of this regret throughout our lives. Surprisingly, the day after his death, we received a cheque for Rs. 60,000/-. What use did the cheque have then? We would not get our father back.

We were helpless. Our family was large and my brothers and sister were so young. The youngest brother was only two years old. My father's friends tried to make us move to our house in the village. At that time, all our neighbours and the Congress Block Members stood by us and gave us strength. We owned about 12 bighas of land at Rampurhat. It was I who told my mother to sell the land so that my elder brother could carry on with father's business. Even today the business that my dada (elder brother) runs is what was started with the money my mother got by selling the land. Many people had told my mother, "You are giving all the money to one son-what will the others do? Suppose this son does not look after you all?" I had told my mother to have faith that dada would look after us all. I still feel proud when I say that what dada has done for the family is exemplary. If the youth of Bengal work hard and sincerely and take up their vocation (whatever be it) in the right spirit, then their efforts will not end up in vain. After my father's death, my dada had taken up the responsibility of the entire family. Today all the brothers and sister have grown up. Apart from the youngest brother, five brothers and my sister have got married. Yet, my dada still supports the family.

I have five nephews and nieces now. Dada's two daughters, Mou and Munni call me "Pumoni", my brothers' sons (Abhishek, Akash and Anklesh) call me "Didi". My younger sister's daughter sometimes comes over and stays with us. Apart from them, there is Seema and Lakhmi. When they were very young, I had brought them over from my village. Today Seema is my constant companion. he stays awake till I return, however late it may be. They are very much members of our family.

I stay preoccupied with politics all the time. That is why the family members do not get any rest when I am in Calcutta. It is most painful for them when people come to me at the middle of the night or at dawn because they need some urgent help. My mother does not get the chance to sleep properly because of this. There is no objection from them (family) in view of the nature of work I have taken up. Such a long time has passed by, but now my mother feels that I will not be allowed to live on. she fears constantly.

Let me come back to politics. The date-31.10.1984. The time-1.30 p.m. The heartbreaking news of Indira Gandhi's assassination arrived. We were with Rajivji at Midnapore on that day. Rajivji halted his tour and returned. In the evening, the official announcement was made. Our Bharat Ratna Indiraji was no more. It was a day of deep anguish for the whole nation-but the Congress Party has one speciality. At the hour of crisis of the nation, the party stands united. That is why, Rajivji took the oath of office as Premier after being elected by the party. Then came the nation-wide 8th General Elections. Jadavpur was the citadel of the Communists. The stalwarts of the party were not willing to contest from Jadavpur. My name was proposed-what could I do? Rashid Gazi from Bishnupur said-"You will have to contest from Jadavpur-we don't want anyone else." At last I submitted my nomination paper as the Congress candidate for Jadavpur constituency. I did not enter the fray with the confidence that I would win-but I was determined not to give up an inch without fight. In the end I won-the red citadel crumbled. Behind my electoral victory was the important role of the common man. If I deny this, I will be telling lie about what is a historical fact. The common man's affection carved out my entry into national level politics-there was also the selfless love and affection of the people of Jadavpur. I shall remain grateful to them throughout my life.

There was another person (a person who had lived the life of a saint throughout and was nearly at the end of his life's circle) whom I did not meet during the election, but who was constantly present at Jadavpur without my knowledge. Many may not know it, but Prafullada (Prafulla Sen) compaigned for me. He would move about Jadavpur on a rickshaw with the microphone tied to it. Khukudi used to accompany him. After winning in the election I rushed to his residence at Middleton Road to seek his blessings. The day, when I first met the Ex-Chief Minister of West Bengal, I realised, what an extra-ordinary man he was. The man who lived on others' generosity and in another person's flat, had never done anything for himself. Here was an ideal person. Such persons are examples to follow in politics, I was amazed. Prafullada blessed me wholeheartedly. He also said, "Mamata, I have crossed the age of ninety. If I had been younger I would have made another attempt (at politics). When I see you I see the light of hope." I still remember Prafullada urging me to eat something. Then he gave me a silk saree and told Khukudi to ask me to wear the saree and show him. He was elder to me, so it was not possible for me to disobey him. Yet, he did not know that I had stopped wearing silk saree after entering active politics. I just could not make him understand. Then I sought Khukudi's help. I told her, "Khukudi, please explain to him that I shall wear it later on." It was because of Khukudi that I got away that day. After that, I used to go to Prafullada every week and listen to his advice. He would express his regret quite often and say, "Mamata, my biggest mistake in life was in bringing the CPI(M) to power and I want to atone for this mistake. I did not realise then that I was bringing in a reptile. This gives me so much mental agony, I cannot explain. I only wonder when they will go out of power. I don't know whether I shall be able to witness their fall." To me he seemed to be really conscience-stricken. Prafullada died on the day of Sasthi Puja in the year 1990. I had not thought that Prafullada would live to be 100 years old. I have seen him giving me so much affection. I have perceived him not only as a political figure, but as a magnanimous person. I remember, I had gone to Arambagh to attend a party meeting in1989. Prafullada was at his residence in Arambagh on that day-somehow, he had come to know that I would be observing the rituals of Mangalchandi on that day. I have observed this ritual on all Tuesdays in the month of Jaistha from an early age. I suddenly saw a note that he had sent through someone. The note said, "Mamata, I know you will be observing Mangalchandi today. You will not be able to eat food bought from the market. I will keep cucumbers and puffed rice for you. On your way back drop in at my house and eat something and then return home". That day I had thought that this is the same Prafullada whom the Leftist "friends" had referred to as inhuman, by various ways and means. What he had said at that time was stark reality and just for the sake of seizing power, so many distorted interpretations were made. Yet, nobody was allowed to know the real Prafullada whose sense of human values wakes the human conscience.

While writing about my life's realisations and experiences, I repeatedly remember Prafullada's supine body after his death and on the other hand his visit to S.S.K.M. Hospital when I was fighting at death's door after being hit at Hazra junction on 16th August. I had heard from my colleagues that Prafullada had put his hand on my head and had gone downstairs when journalists asked him for his comments. He had replied, "Let God give my remaining days to Mamata." That is why, when Prafullada's body lay there lifeless, I rushed over as soon as I got the news although I was ill. I was thinking at that time, "Has Prafullada given up his life to save mine?" I don't know why I had felt guilty. I was thinking-these are the political personalities who are incomparable. Their idealism plants the seeds of sense of values in politics. He will always have a place of great honour in my mind. As long as I live, I will remember Prafullada time and again. His last dreams were to remove the CPI(M) from power and, thus, make amends. Although he could not see this happening in his life-time, we shall fulfil his wish-that is a pledge. That day his soul will find peace and his blessings will shower down invisible to the human eye.

I will revert to the main point. The clash started in a different way this time. Apart from the CPI(M), some from our own party were of the jealous type and they declared that although I had become an MP, Rajiv Gandhi would not come to know of me, even in five years. At that time they did not know that one has to have a distinctive personality and publicity alone cannot make a person known to others. If a person has 10% ability, it can be projected as 12%, but you cannot raise a person from zero to 12. When my career as an MP commenced, I was like an untried fresher. Allegations were made about my educational degree in such a manner as though I had not studied upto the infant grade even and could not even write my own name properly. The identity of the master-minds behind the conspiracy and leaders of this gang are known to me. I do not want to harm or hurt anyone personally, hence I am not mentionning any names of the Left and the Right. Some even tried for the cancellation of my parliamentary membership. At that time I received the endless affection of Rajivji. He protected me like an elder brother. One day while I was sitting morosely and very quietly inside Parliament, a bearer came and said, "The PM has called you urgently." I was dumbstruck. I was just a beginner, why was Rajivji calling me? Had I done something wrong? Such questions flashed through my mind. I went to Rajivji and he surprised me by saying, "Some selfish giants are trying to malign you. Don't be scared. I am here. Whatever help you need-tell me about it. Another thing-I am making you the General Secretary of the All India Youth Congress." I had not worked with the Youth Congress unit before. Whatever be it, the persons who had hoped that my parliamentary membership would be cancelled, were now more incensed.

I started to speak in Parliament about the problems of the people of Bengal, the handing over of unconditional deeds to the refugees, the problems of the employees of the closed factories, the torture on women and the problem of unemployment. I spoke about the different problems and against the CPI(M). At one point MPs of the CPI(M) even said that next time they would not let me win in the elections. Sometimes it was a protest regarding the victims of the adulterated oil scandal, sometimes regarding the retrieval of bodies of victims from the Himalayas-for every such problem I have received all out help from Rajivji. The critics of Rajivji perhaps do not know how simple, innocent and hardworking he was. He loved the new generation deeply.

I remember one incident. The then Chief Minister of Haryana, Devi Lal's grandson's wife had been murdered under mysterious circumstances. I used to attend to my parliamentary work as seriously as a school student. On that particular occasion however, I had been held up at Calcutta for some work and could not reach Delhi on Monday. Next day I rushed to Parliament straight after getting down from the train. A number of members started to ask me why I had not come the day before. I asked, "Why-what has happened?" The Congress MPs said that Devi Lal's grandson's wife had been murdered, but the issue was not raised with enough impact-I would have to do it that day. I raised the issue during zero hour and demanded a CBI enquiry. Let alone supporting me, the leftist and opposition members started to interrupt me. I used to wear a silver bangle at that time. I removed it from my hand and placed it before Madhu Dandavate's table and told, "If none of you have the guts, then wear this bangle." An MP of the TDP left his shoe on my seat. There was tremendous uproar in the House. Afterwards, I went back to my residence and went to sleep after a meal. It was nearly 3 in the night when the telephone rang. As soon as I lifted the phone, I was amazed to hear Rajivji's voice from the other end. He congratulated me over the phone and told me, "You have saved the honour of women today. Fight it out more actively with the people who had left the shoe on your seat." He had noticed what was going on, where and when, in spite of his busy schedule. Can this be forgotten?

Another incident-Priya Ranjan Das Munshi was then the President of the State Unit of the Congress, but I was not able to agree with him over the Block Committees within my own constituency. So, the Committees were not being constituted and it was becoming very difficult to work. I went to Rajivji. He was sitting inside the Lok Sabha and it was around 12-30 p.m. He was scheduled to leave for Amethi shortly afterwards. Whenever he would see me, he used to ask about everything. He would notice everything. Sometimes he would say, "Mamata, why are you losing weight?" At other times he used to say, "You are putting on weight." As soon as I would go to him he would ask me, "What has happened-"Is something wrong?" This time I replied "Please tell Priyada to let me have my say over the Blocks under my constituency, otherwise I am not able to work." I had thought that since he was leaving for Amethi then, he would look after the matter after his return. What a surprise! When I met Priyada in the Central Hall of Parliament around 1 p.m., he said, "Hey, you have complained about me to Rajivji. Whatever you want, just tell me." After that I had no more problems. Things went according to my wishes.

As long as Rajivji was alive, he kept me under his shelter and protection like a banyan tree. At every step, he extended the helping hand and the humane touch. I shall not forget that Rajivji had wanted to appoint me as the Youth Congress President of West Bengal in 1987-88. Again that opposition. Rajivji had arrived from Delhi to inaugurate the Panchayati Raj Project. We had come with him and would be returning with him. I sensed the conspiracy as I entered the aircraft. I saw that some of the leaders of Bengal had gone inside Rajivji's cabin and were discussing with him. After they came out, I was called inside. On entering the cabin I saw that Rajivji was discussing something with Oscar Fernandes (General Secretary, AICC). Seeing me he said, "Mamata, you are doing your work so well and you are working so hard. I want to give you higher responsibilities." Almost immediately I answered, "Rajivji, I don't want anything. I am grateful for what you have told me, but I shall not work in the Mahila Congress Unit." Rajivji understood that I was aware that just before this, people had begged him to stop my appointment as the Youth Congress President. He replied, "Allright, I shall not give you any responsibility which you do not want."

I lost in the 1989 elections. Rajivji felt very sad. After this, my trips to Delhi came to a halt. The agitation against the bus fare hike was at its height. Three persons were killed in police firing.

Agitation had reached everywhere. The police and cadres (refers to the CPI(M) workers) were conspiring together to kill me. I was under survellience, and Rajivji came to know of this. On 12th August, 1990 I suddenly received a phone call from Rajivji's personal secretary, George. George told me, "Can you come to Delhi tomorrow? Rajivji is very worried about you-he wants to talk to you." I explained to him that Congress had announced a general strike on 16th August. So I had to come back the next night. George assured me that it was allright. Immediately after reaching Delhi I went to Rajviji. He said, "I have come to know that they want to kill you. Tell me, how I can help you." In reply I told him that I was truly overwhelmed and that I wanted only his blessings. Rajivji then brought up the old topic and said, ""I have waited a long time. No more waiting. Take up the responsibility of the Youth Congress in West Bengal."

I returned to Calcutta immediately after this. The incidents of 16th August, 1990 need not be narrated again. Everybody knows about it. The details were reported by the newspapers, but I as a witness have not had the opportunity to let everyone know the developments that led to it and about what I came to learn. Prior to 16th August, 1990, the police cars used to follow me whenever I used to go out of my house. They used to keep watch on my destination, my activities and to whom I was talking.

It was just like what life would be in a state of emergency. I recall (the date is probably the 11th August, 1990) that I had gone out to visit Amtala (Bisnupur). I noticed a police car keeping watch over me. I decided that I would not let the police know of my destination. I would go to the party office at Haridevpur to meet Subhasish instead of going to the planned destination. We took the jeep there and I sat inside the party office for a long time. I noticed that the police men were not leaving, so I made a plan. I went to a neighbour's house to drink water. At that time the police reported over their wireless, "Mamata Banerjee has gone inside a house just now-we saw her drinking water." It was like a sports commentary from the grounds. My movements were being relayed in front of me.

Then I told one of my colleagues, "We would have to teach the police a lesson because thay were spying on us. We would have to hoodwink them. They must not know of our plans." I told a colleague to wear a saree like mine and get up on the jeep fast so that the police would think that I was going away-but I would be sitting in the room. The police started to follow the jeep like fools. They had walked into the trap we had laid out. Then I went with Subhasish to the place where I had my work in an autorickshaw. The police used to keep watch over me in this fashion, but they could never unearthen our plans of action. Naturally, the CPI(M) and the police were getting angrier with me. I used to receive threats also at times (e.g. "You will be killed"). A section of the adminstration had warned me to be careful before 16th August-they had warned that there was a conspiracy to kill me, but I had not felt scared. Fear never entered my mind. I had flashed through the newspapers that the CPI(M) and police were planning to kill me.

Then came 16th August. Congress had called for the general strike in West Bengal (on that day) to protest the deaths of Raghunandan, Manas Banerjee and Bimala in police firing. My mother was scared, and she was constantly telling me the night before, "You must not go out tomorrow. They will finish you." I had lied when I reassured her that I would not go out. I had called for the procession and if I did not turn up, then it would be my defeat. So I had to go. I had to resort to some amount of deception. Whenever I go out for any work, it is my habit to see my mother's face and then go out. That day, my mother would not allow me to go out under any circumstances, so when I was getting ready to go out after my taking bath, mother immediately asked, "Where are you going?" I had no other option, I did something which I seldom do-I lied when I told her, "Nowhere-I will be sitting in the office." As soon as my mother had gone inside the house, I alongwith Dilip Majumdar and Anil Mukherjee (Councillor) went out with the boys in a procession. After walking through many streets when we had just crossed the Hazra junction, I saw the armed CPI(M) cadres charging at us with me as the target. Initially I had not understood it all. Many people do not know of what I heard later on from an eye-witness, Kalyan Banerjee, an advocate and whom I know well. Kalyan had been coming towards Hazra and he had taken shelter in a shop when be heard of the trouble there. He saw everything. This is what I heard directly from him. At first, just like in the Hindi movies, young men in four or five taxis started swinging their guns and iron chains at the people and chased them away from the area and took control of it so that there would be no witnesses and nobody would be there to help us. This was the scene before the attack. Then they attacked the procession from the front. My colleagues then pulled me upto the Bata shop opposite the Radhakrishna Temple at Hazra. There I saw Lalu Alam with others coming towards me. They were carrying guns and thick wooden sticks. It was as though I was mentally prepared, that is why I looked at them without any feeling of nervousness. At first, when Lalu Alam struck my head hard with a stick, I felt the blood pouring out profusely from my head and it made my saree wet. After being hit so hard on the head, I was feeling that somebody else had probably taken up my pain. I noticed at that time that the helmet and stick were just like the ones used by the police; I thought, "Is it a joint agreement between the police and the CPI(M)?" Another blow struck as I was thinking. The right side of my head (just a hairline away from where the brain is) had cracked open and I was bleeding profusely. I was still undeterred. I was trying to see what their goal was. When I saw them getting ready to hit me on the head with an iron rod, strangely, in that grave circumstance, I covered by head with my hands. It was such a hard blow that my wrist was nearly crushed. After that I do not know what happened. When I regained consciousness, I discovered that I was in a hospital. Later on I saw in the newspapers that attempts were made to shoot me. A police officer, Gurupada Som had intervened; it must have been this and the affection and blessings of the people which saved me from the jaws of death and the hands of the demon. If I had not been shifted from PG Hospital (by the decision of the party and my family), a plan was there either to kill me or to turn me into a mad person. This is what I heard from a leftist leader [not of the CPI(M)].

Three press photographers were severely beaten up when they were taking my photos on that day. They are Tarapada Banerjee of Ananda Bazar, Partho Sengupta of PTI and photo-journalist Pallab Basu Mallick. The incident had occured in the presence of many policemen at Hazra crossing. Yet, they were like dumb wooden dolls who were witnessing a streetside drama.

It was as though a rehearsal for a drama was going on. Tell me, unless there are directions from the higher ups, can such incidents happen in broad daylight and in front of the administration can be be looked upon as something which is simple and ordinary? It cannot be. This was a conspiracy to throttle the voice of democrcy by those people who sing most about the virtues of democracy. That day, if I had felt scared, I would not have survived. It was the people's love and mental strength which brought me back from the hands of death.

Our beloved leader, Rajivji bore the expenses of my medical treatment. He had sent a messenger to ask me whether I wanted to go to USA for treatment. Long after the incident when I went to see him at Delhi, he was almost childish in his anxiety when he wanted to see the places where I had been hurt. I was under medical treatment when I had come to know that Rajivji had appointed me as the president of the West Bengal Youth Congress. The All India Youth Congress President, Ramesh Chennithala had joined hands with many from West Bengal and did not wish to give me charge of the West Bengal Youth Congress. I have heard that Chennithala had gone to Rajivji with flowers on 20th August (Rajivji's birthday). Immediately on seeing him, Rajivji had told him to go and prepare "Mamata's appointment letter" first and then meet him.

The conspiracies had continued. There were continuous attempts to stop the endorsement of my name in Youth Congress Committee. We also rushed to Rajivji. He took the list (of the committee) from my hand, glanced through it and endorsed it himself; then he handed the list over to George and told him to pass it on to PTI. I shall never forget, I cannot forget how Rajivji saved me from one conspiracy and another.

On 6th May, 1991, Rajivji came to West Bengal for

election meetings. That was 15 days before his death. From the Airport Hotel he came to the Press Club for a conference. Everybody was trying to make Rajivji attend their own meetings. He asked for the list of Meeting immediately after the Press Conference. He saw the list and said, "I will first go to Mamata's meeting and then to the others". He was tired, his voice was hoarse and there was hardly any personal security. He swept like a storm through the ocean of people-all this I had seen.

He came to my meeting at Deshapriya Park. It was 9 p.m. Even at that hour the crowd looked like an ocean. Traffic had stopped on Rashbehari Avenue and Lansdowne Road. People were mad to catch a glimpse or just to be able to touch him once. At the meeting there was a glass of warm water in front of him. He was taking a sip of the water, clearing his throat and resuming his speech. He spoke for about half an hour. Immediately after finishing his speech he called me aside on the rostrum. Then he asked me, "How are you?" He put his hand on my head and blessed me and then he seemed to be borne away by the assembled mass to the next meeting place. I had watched his departure steadfastly, a premonition of the dangers ahead had shaken my mind. He was not at all worried about his own safety; what if something happens-I thought over and again. "Is this the last time that I have seen him".

Then-21st May, 1991-10.20 p.m.-the most horrifying bomb blast of the century at Sreeperampudur. He left us, his blood marking his victory over death-the immortal youth. Since my father's death, this was the second time that I was left without a guardian. I could not speak to anyone for seven days, I could not eat. I had closed the door of my room and just wept. In the strains of the lyre in my life, in every step that I take, at every moment, I feel his presence. Whenever I face any problem or difficulties come in my way, without being aware of it, my gaze goes to his portrait in the room. It seems to me that with a little smile he is saying, "Mamata, how are you? You are not facing any difficulty, are you?"

In 1991, the Lok Sabha and Vidhan Sabha elections were held simultaneously. Sri Siddhartha Sankar Ray was the Pradesh Conress President. Eleven of us were members of the Election Committee. Everyday we held meetings at Manuda's (S.S.Ray) residence. During these meeting I had observed that I would be of one opinion and the others would obviously have some other viewpoint-the Congress leaders of 1977-1990 in a group and I alone on the other side. The reason for this was that, from 1977 to 1990, no new leaders from the younger generation had been given the opportunity to come up. My knowledge of the "Chanakya" intrigues has been always negligible and being a person with a different and newer outlook, I was not acquainted with the many facets of human character. I failed to realise many things. I observed that when each of them spoke to me individually, they would agree with me, but at the meetings they would be totally different.

I woke up one day. One of our Congress leaders was staying at a reputable hotel. He and another esteemed leader rang me up and asked me to join them for an important meeting. I spoke to my colleagues and we felt that I should go-after all they were senior leaders, and if I did not respond, they would say-Mamata is not co-operating, she does not wish well for the party, etc. etc. Reluctantly, I went. We sat down, the leaders on either side of me. One of them told me that Shyamal Chakravarty [of CPI(M)] had suggested that if I accepted his terms, then he would leave my South Calcutta Constituency undisturbed. I asked "What terms?" The terms were that, if the person nominated by me was made the candidate for Manicktolla, which was Shyamal Chakravarty's constituency, the CPI(M) would not allow me to win from South Calcutta. I told both of them to inform the CPI(M) that they could "disturb" me in South Calcutta to their heart's content and also that, it made no difference to me. My candidate would stand for elections from Manicktolla. For the sake of becoming an MP, I would not give up my ideals, nor cast aside my integrity. My sacred duty was to protect this ideal and my belief in truth, both of which I have treasured since childhood and placed on the pristine altar of justice. Now, with the truth revealed, some may do penance for my early demise. I have heard that some persons have even sought shelter with a priest of the Tantric-order!

At first, with the congress flag held high, when I had raised the call "Vande Mataram", impassioned and unfettered from the depth of my soul, I had not imagined that there could exist such harmonious co-relation between the Left and the Right. After this incident, I became cautious, for I had come under the venomous ire of some so-called leaders. I realised that I would be facing tremendous opposition and hostility. To overcome this fearlessly, I would have to strike. I remembered Swamiji's words, in his "Call to The Nation" "Each one thinks his method is the best; but remember, it may be good for you alone. Food which is indisgestible to one is digestible for another, because it is good for you do not jump to the conclusion that your method is everyone's method, that Jake's coat fits John and Mary". I realised that the alliance between the Left and the Right would not suit me. Then started the bitter clash of differing ideals.

In the last election I was unwilling to be a candidate. I had felt, instead of being a candidate, if I had toured entire Bengal and worked for the party candidates, then more seats could be won. However, Rajivji had said, "I want you in Parliament". So I contested. With the people's blessings I won. I received felicitations from many persons; but he, whose well-wishes I wistfully longed for, our beloved leader Rajivji, had left us forever, some days ago. In Delhi, the Ministry was formed under Narsimha Rao's leadership. Believe me, I had never comtemplated being a minister. At that point I was staying at the home of an MP from Bengal. I observed the amount of effort he put in to become a Minister-preparing his bio-data, rushing from person to person with it, even handing it over to the Prime Minister's lackey. Seeing this, I felt he would surely be made a minister. I was at Rajivji's house at 10, Janpath Road, when the swearing-in-ceremony of the Cabinet was taking place. Alongwith Sree George I was watching it on television. Memories of Rajivji kept coming back and I was unable to check the flow of tears. Emotions overcame me, I was unable to stay there any more and I went back to the MP's house where I had been staying. My colleagues greeted me with the news that my name had been announced and I was to go to the Rashtrapati Bhavan. I was quite unprepared for this. My colleagues were urging me to go. Since I was unwilling, I told them, "I do not have a card, protocol has to be maintained at Rashtrapati Bhavan and I do not want to break any." They were adamant and said, "You go and introduce yourself and they will call you inside". I was still in a dilemma. This was the Prime Minister's own selection and I was very much in Delhi. If I did not pay heed, some would construe it as my lack of confidence in him. To abide myself by party discipline, I went. Many persons were pleased when I took the ministerial oath.

I had no experience-would I be able to carry out my duties? With confusing thoughts crowding my mind, I went to Shastri Bhavan. I found everything well-organised there. I even found that there were some persons with whom I was able to establish a rapport-especially with Dharda, Ratanda and Ashok. I received co-operation from all the staff members. I was able to work unhindered because of this. I was in charge of the Sports, Youth, Women and Child ministry, a small ministry, but having wide-spread opportunities for work. On one side were my ministerial duties and on the other, Bengal's political scenario-the daily happenings of torture and murder, the people's grief at losing their dear ones, their sorrowful cry. My thoughts were pervaded with Bengal and subconciously, my mind would call out, "My precious Bengal, I love you".

I was a minister for one year, five months and had tried my best during this tenure. During the Budget debate, inspite of being a minister, I constantly raised the question in Parliament-Why was "sports and Youth welfare' not treated as a matter of "national interest"? I had placed before Parliament the actual state of affairs concerning national sports. I felt that the participation of government and non-government agencies were needed for the formation of a "Sports Academy", it was our moral responsibility to encourage them in various ways to participate in this venture. I have arranged for tax concessions to be given to "investors" in the field of sports. I do not hesitate to profess that the import of sports equipment were made duty-free through my efforts. I had observed that, alongwith the need to honour the economically weak but outstanding sportspersons, was the necessity to send talented but poor children abroad for training-this was arranged. Also, special schemes for the physically handicapped persons were sanctioned during my tenure in the Ministry. My intention was not to let the venemous presence of politics defile the world of sports. In an attempt to rejuvenate the image of Indian Sports in the international arena, I had formed committees with eminent sportspersons and experts as members and had tried to follow their advice always.

I took the initiative of bringing village-sports like Kho-Kho and kabbadi into the mainstream of national sports, talent-scouting for gifted young sportspersons from tribal and backward class backgrounds and then arranging for their training. To improve the tarnished state of Indian sports and develop it on the lines of the Chinese system I sent a team of representatives there. I have never gone on a foreign trip on the pretext of attending the Olympic Games and thus draining government money.

During my tenture the Nehru Youth Centres were revived. The proposal to use the Youth Development Centres for helping youth in character-forming and imparting vocational training to them was mine-the result of this will be evident in the 8th 5 Year Plan.

By enlarging the perimeters of the National Women's Commission, Women's Development Corporation, Adolescent Girls' Scheme and I.C.D.S Programme, I was able to bring within the purview of these organisations the people from scheduled castes and tribes and women from ill-famed areas. I had arranged for the distribution of sports equipment to numerous deserving clubs and youth organisations.

I am fully aware that this is not enough. In fact nobody is perfect. Even with my scant knowledge and perception, I am aware that work can be done if the will to do it exists. I can with conviction say that if all the schemes that I had taken up are successfully adopted, then Indian sports will truly progress. No one had paid much attention to Sports before 1982 i.e. the year of Asian Games. This was the watershed. Rajivji came to power and he re-instated immortal youth as the crown prince again. Youth was once again given it's rightful dues. During his Prime Ministership, in

1986, the Sports and Youth Wing was formed. As foreseen by Rajivji, the importance of Youth and Sports Welfare is boundless in the country's journey towards the 21st century. For this, time, experience and sincerity are needed.

Inspite of the busy ministerial schedule, I had not forgotten Bengal. After all I am from Bengal-"Bengal's soil, Bengal's water, Bengal's atmosphere, Bengal's produce" are my invaluable heritage. "Bengal's soil, Bengal's mind, Bengal's youth" are my soul-mates, all held so dear to me. Whenever people from Bengal have come to me with their pain and sorrow, I have sincerely tried to help them. After the floods in North Bengal, I had rushed with aid from the P.M.'s Relief Fund. While standing beside the stranded tourists from Bengal after the devastating earthquake in Uttarkashi, I had wanted to say only one thing-"I am one of you, let me be known by this identity."

I pray to God, "O, Lord of All, give me strength, give me courage. People are so helpless. Sorrow, pain and misery surround them. Allow me to be sympathetic towards these people." I feel as if I have been able to conquer the world if I can help the grief-stricken and repressed people, and when I am unable to do anything for them I feel miserable and weep; I sit in the darkness and humbly ask God,

> Today my voice is quelled, no music flows from the flute,
>
> My world is lost, dragged in the nightmare,
>
> For this I repay with my tears,
>
> They who have defiled your world and extinguished your light,
>
> Have you forgiven them, have you given them your love?"

Let my prayers be expressed in the words of our great poet, Rabindra Nath Tagore-"Give me the strength never to disown the poor or bend my knees before the insolent might." Let me be able to sincerely feel for the people and share their sorrow. This will be my greatest possession, my life's perception.

In the meantime, many changes had occurred in the political scene. The Pradesh Congress President and Leader of the Congress Party in the Vidhan Sabha, Siddhartha Sankar Ray had suddenly decided to relinquish his post. Who would become President-the speculations started. The election for the President's post became inevitable. In the beginning, I had not contemplated contesting for the post. I observed that some leaders, who were totally unfit for the President's post, were using the newspapers for "promoting" their names. Around this time, I rang up Somenda and asked him, "Are you contesting?" He said, "No". I requested him, "If you contest, please let me know beforehand." Somenda had been the General Secretary of the Pradesh Congress for a long time. When Barkatda had been the President, Somenda had actually been doing his work. Through the years Somenda had held various posts in the Pradesh Congress. As a result, he had his own coterie in the districts. I had become the Youth Congress President barely a year ago. Though I too had had the opportunity to tour the districts, I had not had the inclination to form my own coterie.

The power struggle started. A new drama unfolded in the rat-race for the much desired post. Priyada and many others urged me to contest. I was a Minister at that time. Some well-known persons, connected with the newsmedia, requested me to contest-so that the movement against the CPI(M) rule could be accelerated and the image of the party not allowed to rot away.

Events leading to the election had been much publicised in newspapers. Pranabda was our candidate. I respect him and even today our relationship is that of a brother and sister. He had been pleased when I had won from the Jadavpur constituency. I had been saddened when he was not made a minister in Rajivji's Cabinet. In 1985, as Pradesh Congress President, he had really worked hard. I too had tried to do my best. The day Pranabda was expelled from the party, it was like a nightmare to me. The practice today is-when one wields power, he is much sought after and when he loses power, he is totally ignored by the others. After his expulsion, whenever he went to the Central Hall of the Parliament, he was ignored by all.

One day I had come upon an MP (a self-styled leader) writing a "memorandum", It was a "felicitation message' to Rajivji for having expelled Pranabda from the party. He had come over to me for my signature. I noticed that he had signed first. I asked him, "Who has entrusted you with this work?" Immediately he had resorted to lying and said that Rajivji had asked him to do it. I went to Rajivji and asked him, "Rajivji, have you told someone to collect signatures against Pranab Mukherjee?" Rajivji had truly been an open-hearted person. On hearing this, he had been astounded and said, "No". I went back and took the "memorandum' from" the MP and tore it in front of him. Then I told him, "You can leave. You have just lost the chance of becoming a minister this time".

I have mentioned this incident because I had stood by Pranabda even during his darkest days. Day after day, in full view, I had sat beside him in the Central Hall. Quite openly, I would visit his house. Like the cuckoo which appears during the springtime, there are people who visit persons only during their good spells. I have never been like the cuckoo.

Pranabda formed the Rashtriya Samajbadi Congress, Even then, I had tried to convince Rajivji for taking him back. Whenever I got the opportunity, I would tell Rajivji that Pranabda had been taken wrongly.

Pranabda had been preferred by everyone for the P.C.C. President's post. So, what had happened? why had he started misunderstanding me? In a room in the Steel Guest House on Camac Street, the "election procedures" meeting had been going on. Nearly all the leaders were present. I know for certain that some persons had instigated Pranabda to such an extent that, uncharacteristically, he had misunderstood my intentions and had admonished me. I had never expected such treatment from him. I had gone away hurt and was sad. I had remembered an incident from the past. Once I had been staying at Pranabda's residence-I was not an MP at that time. I had told him, "May be when good times come for you again, I shall not be able to visit you".

I had never imagined that this would become true before the party elections. I had thought-Pranabda was displeased with me. The party elections were going to be held. At first the 20 District Returing Officers were to be appointed and they would have the final say about conducting the elections. They were to prepare the list of Pradesh Committee members from the districts. Hence the appointment list of DROs had been an important factor. When the names of 20 DROs were released, we saw that only 4 of them were from amongst us. Since I used to depend on Pranabda totally, my ire, naturally, was directed at him. From then, the mistrust was born. I wondered-did this mean Pranabda wanted somebody else to be the President and not himself? I had felt angry. I have an adamant streak in me. If anybody convinces me about something, I readily accept it. However. if my feelings are wounded, I cannot accept it. I knew all the powerful Congress leaders of Bengal were ranked against me. Some of them had been in constant touch with the CPI(M) over this issue. Certain businessmen, who are the middlemen for some of the Left and Congress leaders, had been specially enthusiastic.

All this had culminated in a storm! I had decided to let the truth prevail. After all, winning election was not the important thing. What was important was the thrust necessary to change the basic moral character. Even if one lost, in reality, by upholding values, that person would have a moral win. I had contested for the post of the President. Stark circumstances had forced me in the rat-race, a thing which I have always abhorred. Out of the 400 selected PCC members, 34 were from our group. The challenge had been there-best said in Swamiji's inspiring words-"Death is better than a vegetating ignorant life, it is better to die on the battlefield than to live a life of defeat." Besides, there had been the necessity to reveal the true colour of certain persons and to analyse what was wrong and right. Rajivji had told many persons, "Now I want Mamata to take charge." Narsimha Rao, who had been Prime Minister at that time, had also wanted me to win. Yet, some newly cropped-up leaders had tried to prevent this. Coming from a very ordinary financial background, had it been possible for me to meet their various requirements?

I had felt like an abandoned puppet in the midst of a "money-game", a game of deceit and the Left-Right "understanding". Like Abhimanyu (refer to Mahabharata) I had stepped inside the battle-lines. If the PCC membership lists of Darjeeling and Nadia had been published, then in all probability, I would not have lost. It was destined to be so. On hindsight, I realised that I should not have contested. Apparently, it had been a major mistake. Yet, if I had not contested, I would not have had the opportunity to find out

CPI(M)'s interest in the elections, whom they had been interested in, and the reasons for it. Would I have found out about the prior assurances for "winning" Vidhan Sabha seats, the cringing dependence of some persons on CPI(M) for personal gains, or about the persons who were simply jealous of me? Would I have found out about the attempt to put an end to my anti-CPI(M) movement and the midnight meeting with the CPI(M) leaders to prepare the blueprint for my defeat? At the Maharashtra Niwas Hall, where the PCC election was being held, I had been convinced that some of these people would stab me in the back. When I felt despondent about this, I remembered the words of Swamiji-"Never mind these failures, these little backslidings; hold the ideals a thousand times, make the attempt once more." It is true that I had been deeply hurt, saddened and offended, but for the sake of my colleagues and to honour the love given to me by the people of Bengal, I had taken a firm grip on myself and became resolute; after all, "strength is the medicine of the world's disease." Like in a game, there is success and failure in life. Just as there is joy in winning, in failure, one gets the chance to analyse.

Then came the Ballygunge bye-election-a blood-drenched chapter, the murder of democracy. I had worked wholeheartedly for our party candidate, Dibyendu Biswas's win. The campaign had been in full swing. At an election meeting in Picnic Garden, the Chief Minister had announced "a section of the Congress", meaning us, was trying to create disorder. I had a faint hope that the bye-election would be held properly-that the people would be allowed to participate in a fair election. I had been so gullible and naive. After all, the whole game had already been played at Nandan-"Give Behrampur the take Ballygunge." The roots of the Left-Right combine were so deeply embedded; even after being in politics for so long, I had not been able to understand this. This proves how foolish I had been. The Ballygunge bye-election turned into a farce. The people protested. My fellow-workers tried their best. Dibyendu was so naive; he slogged from the morning. Saugatada, Shovanda and Sadhanda worked hard. Pankaj Banerjee was hit when he had protested. Swapan Chakraborty was killed in the police firing and Gariahat Road became blood-drenched. A helpless family-parents lost their son, a wife lost her husband and a baby lost his father. I had not seen through the game and the way in which the give and take policy had gnawed through value based politics. If I had the sense to see through then I would have realised that "a cooked fish cannot move its head'. I came to know about the entire drama from a "third spectator" after a long time. I had asked, "Why hadn't you told me of the "Nandan' drama before the election?" He answered, "I got afraid to speak about it." After the Ballygunge bye-election, we took up the cause of "No identity card, no vote". At that time I was a Union Minister.

For a long time, my colleagues had been wanting me to hold a rally at the Brigade Parade Ground. For ten long years this had not been possible. The Congress had not been in power for many years, popular leaders like Indiraji and Rajivji were no longer alive and the costs went high, above all, whether we would be capable of organising a programme of such gigantic proportion-all these conflicting thoughts had made me hesitant. At a public meeting at Esplanade East, on the spur of the moment, I announced my decision to hold the next meeting at the historic Brigade Parade Ground. This had an electrifying effect on the people. Shedding all apprehensions, depending on the enthusiasm of the party workers and with people's love and support, I started arranging for it. Each time I passed the massive Brigade Ground, I would think-let the meeting not turn out to be a flop. Not only the CPI(M), but many of our party leaders had wanted it to fail. It is true that we received the co-operation of trade unions, all organisations belonging to the Congress and of course the people. From Delhi, Pranabda and Santoshda had extended their help. Santoshda was the only leader from Delhi who had attended the meeting; he had arrived after the meeting was over and we had to resume the meeting so that he could address the crowd.

We started preparing for the meeting. I had personally taken care of the details. I had requested all organisations and trade unions (participating in the meeting) to put up temporary arches at important road-crossings in their neighbourhoods. Pranabda and Santoshda had borne the cost of erecting the dais and the public address system. There had been many attempts to hinder the preparations for the meeting. Inspite of this we had not stopped. A week before the meeting, whole of Bengal had started resounding with the call, "Brigade Chalo". It was beyond imagination that a meeting at Brigade could be arranged by spending so little. There was enthusiasm everywhere. The preparations for the meeting had started in full swing-the dias was being built, tri-colour flags were being strung across the entire ground and the surrounding areas, there were discussions going on with the fellow-workers, the distribution of leaflets and posters had been started, staying arrangements for the people coming from the districts were being made and touring the districts to invite the people to participate was taken up. I had been infused with enthusiasm.

It had rained heavily the day before the meeting. Feeling dejected, I had rushed to the Brigade Ground. Nothing had stopped there. It had seemed that preparations for a festival were going on. I had thought of the saying-"If winter comes, can spring be far behind?" On

25th November, there had been no sign of rain, Only the dazzling sunshine beckoning the people to go to the Brigade Ground. I had been filled with joy. There had been one lingering worry-if the crowd would be enough to fill up the Brigade Ground? At 12.30 p.m., when I had arrived at the meeting, with a group of persons who had suffered in the hands of the CPI(M), there had been a crowd of nearly fifty thousand people. Gradually it swelled. It had appeared that all roads of Bengal were pointing towards the Brigade Ground. Within an hour the crowd had spilled over, like a huge wave. Even then, the number of people still coming in, had seemed countless. I had thought-was this a dream or a mirage? By then Priyada and Somenda had already finished addressing the crowd. The call "Vande Mataram" was resounding all over the grounds. I had felt hurt that only Santoshda had come from Delhi to attend the meeting. I had been caught in an emotional maelstrom-such were my feelings that I had started shivering. I had thought-the huge crowd, the people who had come from far-flung places, carrying the Congress flag, the people who got their backs pushed against the wall tortured by the CPI(M), they who had nothing more to lose, they who would go back to their homes with the death-toll of the CPI(M) ringing in their ears-I had to give them a message that would revive and enthuse them to fight back the CPI(M). I had always been conscience-stricken by the fact that, I had been a minister. At that point I had realised that the overwhelming love of the people that had united me with them, was far above any ministerial post and I had to honour this love. Seeing the crowd that had come to ring the death-knell of the CPI(M), I had realised that the people were no longer able to bear the torture in the hands of the CPI(M). The tears of the people, their distress, their grief at the loss of dear ones while standing there on the dais, these thoughts had struck me and had shaken the very depth of my soul. It was at that point of time that I had made up my mind. To make the sound of the death-toll of the CPI(M) to reach all corners of Bengal, from Canning to Kanchanjungha, the shackles of the ministerial responsibility had to be shed off; I would have to stay in Bengal. I had astounded everyone by announcing my resignation from the ministership from the dais that day. While many persons had been pleased, others had been saddened. Santoshda had not arrived when I made the announcement; if he had reached on time, or had learnt of my decision beforehand, he would not have allowed me to resign. The sudden resignation had led to a lot of debate and criticism. Since the decision to resign had entirely been mine, it was my responsibility to explain.

Actually, I had to offer something to the people. Whatever I have received in life, the hope that had illuminated the path to where I stood then and the main inspiration had all come from the people. I had to give back something to them. Believe me-there had been a storm hammering at the door of my soul telling me, if I was to dedicate myself to the people, then I had to give up something. Yet, I did not have much to give. The amount of love, trust and blessings that I had received from the people, could not be repaid. My ministerial post-that had also been a gift from the people. Therefore, as a gesture of thanks-giving, I had laid down that post at the doors of the people's court.

Alongside, this had been a test for me. Was it easy to wear the crown, but hard to give it up? Did having power mean only enjoying its fruits? If necessary some sacrifices had to be made. Power can not be a constant factor in an individual's life.

It had been necessary to test whether I could give up the "luxury" of holding power and work beside the people as one of them. Also, I had to find out whether the persons who were constant companions when I held power in my hands, would remain so when I relinquished it. On the one hand was the gradual erosion of Bengal's economy, and on the other, the murders, terror, torture and oppression. Yet, no one was bothered. Someone had to remain beside the people constantly and with sincerity, like a sentinel. Love for the people made me give up my ministerial post and I assumed the role of the sentry.

Meanwhile the "wave of humanity" was so huge, the Brigade Ground appeared to vibrate. Procession after procession had still been coming in. The crowd was so massive that a part of the dais was crushed. Innumerable men and women everywhere; the children had literally suffocated in the rush. The important Leftist leader, Jatin Chakravorty (who had joined the meeting) had been sitting on a chair, on the dais. At one point I turned my head back-there was only the crowd and Jatinda alongwith his chair was no longer there! The "cultural" dias and the dais meant for the "oppressed people' had started collapsing. Over the wireless of the police, reports had been coming in that even then, people were pouring in at procession Sealdah and Ballygunge railway stations. I had thought-I would be getting other opportunities for addressing meetings, but at the moment I could not allow the people who had come to die in stampede. For this reason I had hastily announced the end of the meeting. While I was making my announcement, I heard the sirens-Santoshda had arrived. He had got stuck in processions and had not been able to reach on time. As soon as he had arrived, I resumed the meeting. Even then the flood of people coming in had not ended. Santoshda addressed the crowd and the meeting ended with his speech. I had been anxious-whether the people who had come to the meeting would be able to reach their homes safely?

It had appeared that the "masters" of the Adminstration had vanished into thin air after witnessing the spontaneity of the people. A large number of people had passed by the Writers' Buildings on vehicles and on foot, in processions; yet, nobody had been guarding it. People had come in lakhs, but they had been so calm and had quietly left after the meeting. In the same manner, one day, the silent humanity will agitate and wrench power from the oppressors.

After our 25th November meeting, the CPI(M) had decided to retaliate with a Brigade meeting. At Government's cost, with its support, the preparations were started. Lakhs of rupees were spent. The licences of the rickshaw-pullers and cart-pullers were impounded, trade-licenses were snatched away from shop-keepers, ration cards were taken away from the ration shops and deposited at the CPI(M) local committee offices. Some senior police officers [who obey dictates of the CPI(M)] had also joined in to ensure the success of the meeting. I have heard that, some of these officers had forcibly stopped passing lorries, herded poor people in these lorries and had compelled them to go to the meeting.

That day I had been on my way to the Pradesh Congress Office for a Press Conference. A CPI(M) procession had been passing by and my colleagues travelling with me in the car had said, "You should not have come out now, they may attack you." By then some of the processionists had recognised me. They told me, "Didi, we have been forced to join the procession; for the sake of our lives we have joined. If we don't join, we will not get back our tokens." At that moment, I had realised that the days (of staying in power) were numbered for the CPI(M) and the death-knell had really rung for them.

By then the death-knell had started ringing all over

Bengal. The CPI(M) were torturing our party workers because they had attended our meeting. At this juncture, on 6th December, '92, the conflagration of communalism had spread across the country. The BJP had demolished the Babri Masjid. For a long time a conspiracy had been growing to start a bloodbath in the country in the name of religion. The communal riots had started. Though we all know who were the persons responsible for the riots in Bengal, I am not mentioning the names. I still believe that the Central Government should not have believed the assurances given by the BJP and should have taken the necessary precautions. Both the Congress and the CPI(M) had called for a Bangla Bandh (General Strike) on 7th December, '92. Our protest procession started from Subodh Mullick Square; on reaching the foot of Gandhiji's statue, we had pledged to safeguard secularism. I had observed some very rough looking youths trying to obstruct the procession from moving on. Somenda had been on his way to join the meeting and these youngmen had demonstrated in front of his car. I had requested a doctor, who is known to me, to take me back home in her car. Somehow, I went back home after the meeting. In the meantime, phonecalls had started pouring in there-people's frantic pleas from Garden Reach, Topsia, Tangra, Tiljala, Beckbagan and Park Circus. After reaching home, I sat in my office answering these calls, with Manik Majumdar, my longtime associate and co-worker. It is hard to find such a genuine and trustworthy person. He takes care of my office. He does not leave for his home until I return, however late I may be.

During the riots I had kept vigil throughout the nights, contacting the authorities whenever any news of rioting was relayed to me. Therefore, Manik had not been able to go back home. Each evening I used to go round the riot-affected areas, trying to find out the problems. I had realised then how weak the authority was-merely tin-soldiers. People were being killed, there was wide-spread arson, houses were being set on fire, people were tortured-all this had been going on unchecked. This made one wonder whether a government had been in existence! When I had realised that the Administration would not be capable of controlling the riots, I rang up Sharad Pawar from my office, who had been Defence Minister then. Priyada, Saugatada and Dilip had been with me then. I requested Sharadji to deploy troops to Calcutta immediately. I had also informed the Prime Minister about what had been happening in Calcutta. If the military had not stepped in that day in Calcutta, I doubt whether the blaze could have been put off!

Around this time, one day we had gone to meet the Chief Minister. Our appeal had been that setting aside political differences, everyone should work together to restore peace. He had informed that Special Cells had been formed at Writers' Buildings and Lal Bazar (Police HQ) and any news regarding the riots had to be conveyed there. Accordingly, we had sent all the informations to those cells. I remember, one night I had to repeatedly ring up Lal Bazar. I had been trying to tell them that rioting had broken out in a certain area. The Duty Officer of the Special Cell in Lal Bazar told, "People die in riots. Why are you persistently pestering us?" This had proved, to what height arrogance had taken the "authorities" to.

A particular incident had deeply affected me. An elderly Muslim from Hoogly, who had been working in Calcutta, had been severely beaten up while returing home with his son. He had been admitted to P.G. Hospital with serious injuries. After hearing this, I had rushed to the hospital. The man was fighting with death. Seeing this, my inner being had sobbed-were the persons responsible for the old man's condition not aware that any incident could not be avenged by such acts? It can never be so. Despite all efforts, the old man died. In similar manner, many persons had died during the riots and many had become homeless. Wherever possible, I had tried to help. I had appealed to Smt. Sonia Gandhi for help and arrangements were made and stoves, tarpaulins, hurricane-lamps, utensils, clothes, food and medicine were distributed. Though I know this had not been enough to help all the people, I had not been able to sit back doing nothing. Even today people come to me, who having lost everything during the riots, are yet to receive minimum compensation from the Government. The persons who had started the riots and spread the poisonous vapours of communalism in Calcutta are yet to be punished, Patronised by the political hobnobs, they enjoy life and dream of a golden future. I do not think they will ever be brought to trial.

Gradually the riots subsided and normalcy was restored. Then came the incident at Writers' Buildings on 7th January, 93. A woman from Nadia, Phelani Basak, had been in touch with me. Her fourteen year old mute daughter, Dipali, had been ravished by a cadre of the CPI(M) party, and she became pregnant. Being dumb, she had not been able to tell anyone of her plight. By the time her mother came to know of what had happened, it was already too late. She had come rushing to me for help. At that time the Chief Minister of West Bengal and his family were taking a holiday at Ganga Sagar, Believe me, on 7th January, '93, the day he had returned from his holiday, I had tried to contact him on telephone at least ten times. I wanted to tell him about the incident and ask for redressal for the girl. At that time I had been a Central Minister. I had sought an appointment, even if it was for merely two minutes. With great reluctance the Writers' Buildings had informed, "You can visit. If the C.M.! comes, then we'll arrange for the appointment." I had thought if the C.M. did not attend his office that day, then I would ask Sovanda (MLA) to take the helpless mother and daughter to the Chief Secretary and tell him everything. I had reached Writers' Buildings at about 3 P.M. I told Sovanda, "I am waiting in the Press Corner. You inform the Chief Minister's PA/CA that we have come and request them to spare some time for us". Sovanda had come back and informed me that the C.M.'s secretary had behaved very improperly with him. Just imagine, a legislator being insulted at Writers' Buildings because he had gone there to seek an appointment with C.M. I had told Sovanda, "We have not come to the C.M. seeking personal favours. We have accompanied a helpless girl, asking for justice. Will justice cry in solitude? I am waiting in the Press Corner. You go alongwith the unfortunate mother and daughter and sit in protest in front of the C.M.'s room as a sign of protest". Even then I had not imagined that circumstances would force me also to go there. While I was waiting, I had suddenly heard that a huge police contingent had arrived to drag away the mother and daughter in a bid to suppress the truth. When I had heard this, I had been unable to remain just sitting. I could not accept the fact that a dumb, innocent pregnant girl, seeking justice at Writers' Buildings would be further humiliated at Writers' Buildings itself. I had rushed there and told the policemen, "Don't you have shame and self-respect? It's not that I haven't informed and come. Though the C.M. is in Calcutta, can't he spare just two minutes? To him I may be an "inferior girl', (quoting the C.M.) but is there no human feeling left in this world? Then I had seen a policeman come running. He had said, "Madam, please wait. The C.M. has arrived and he will meet you". While he had been saying this, I saw the C.M. striding by and entening his chamber. To tell the truth, if we had wanted to stop him that day, we could have done that. However, that had not been our intention. I had thought-such a far-reaching incident; the entire Writers' Buildings in a turmoil, surely the C.M. would listen to helpless girl and her mother, even if he did not meet us.

No, I was disproved. Following the C.M. had come some pompous, intellectual persons. They distorted the facts. Instructions were then sent from the C.M.'s room to forcibly remove us from Writers' Buildings. The policemen had leaped into action. Alongwith the huge contingent on duty at Writers' Buildings, some very servile officers of the anti-rowdy squad had then dragged us down, beating us, from the second floor of the building to the ground floor. The photographers from the news media, who had been present, were also beaten up when they had tried to film what was happening. Their cameras were broken. Some of the government employees who had been present, were not spared. After that, we had been arrested and taken to Lal Bazar (Police HQ). By then, I was having stomach cramps and my arms were paining badly. They had wrenched my arms and had kicked me in the stomach. Dipali's body was twisting and turning in pain. From there I had contacted Ramkrishna Mission Seva Pratisthan for her emergency treatment. The missionaries and doctors from there had treated her with utmost care, free of cost, and had helped her to get a bit well. We were kept in Lal Bazar. To tell the truth, till then, nobody had treated us badly at Lal Bazar. By then we had started our protest fast inside the lock-up. At about midnight, I lay down alongwith a few of my colleagues, thinking that nobody would disturb us during the rest of the night. At 12.30 a.m., I had heard the rattling of the door. I said, "Why are you disturbing us so late in the night ? We do not trust you. We will not open the door." Then I heard the voice of a police officer who had a conscience and sense of values and was a gentleman.

Hearing his voice, I had to open the door. Apologetically he had said, "Didi, forgive me. I had given my word that I would not disturb you during the night, but I am helpless. There are instructions from the top to remove you, at any cost, from Lal Bazar during the night. I am unable to do this unjust act. So, I am going on leave. I cannot carry the burden of this wrong doing".

Then a group of frenzied, drunk policemen had come in. Shamelessly, they had started shoving and pushing us. To protect our self-dignity, we had somehow got out of the room and went to the main-gate where we sat down to show our protest. Then some arrogant police officers had ordered lathi-charge and firing. A group of policemen had said that they would not participate in such a mischievous act. The eagerly waiting non-gazetted policemen, having CPI(M) affiliations, had then jumped into action. They had started beating us mercilessly. My women colleagues were struck on the head. The police knew I had a head injury-this is a weak spot, so they targetted my head. If two of my colleagues had not shielded me with their bodies from the demented blows that were being aimed at my head, I do not know what would have been the consequences. A few well-wishing policemen had told me, "Didi, they have planned to kill you, please go away from here. If they kill you, then we will be finished". Outside, the journalists had been waiting in apprehension, fearing that something terrible would happen. I had thought-here is a group of intoxicated policemen with homicidal tendencies-how can I expect any civilised behaviour from them ? So, we came out of Lal Bazar. The police had followed us till Mayo Road. On reaching the foot of Gandhiji's statue on Mayo Road, that cold winter night, I had taken the oath-as long as the arrogant Chief Minister Jyoti Basu remains in power, I will neither see his face nor put my foot inside Writers' Buildings.

There had been a general demand for a Bandh the next day. I had not agreed because it would have caused inconvenience to the common man. For a long time certian persons had been conspiring to stifle the voice of the news media. After the 7th January incident had been flashed in all the newspapers with the revealing photographs, the press corner in Writers' Buildings was demolished. Severe rules were imposed restraining the unrestricted and rightful movements of the newspersons by the Second-In-Command of the Left Front and his colleagues. This has been branded as the greatest blow to the newsmedia in the annals of democracy.

Even after this incident, I had been astounded at the total silence of the central leaders, who had remained like "mute saints". I was hurt. Though ours had been a minority government, a token protest by the party leadership had been necessary at that time. May be the necessity to stay in power had stifled the voice of protest. Of course, I had not expected anything more. Some central ministers had run up to enquire. After realising the gravity of what had happened, a Working Committee member (Congress) had wanted to meet me. I had told him on the telephone, "It is too late". On 18th January my resignation from the ministry was accepted. I was freed from the shackles.

After this came the Tripura Vidhan Sabha election. Dejected and unwell, I had made up my mind not to go anywhere. Suddenly, one day there was a message from the PMO saying that the Prime Minister would be going to Guwahati and I was to go there and meet him. I was to join the election campaign. Since I could not refuse the P.M., I went to Meghalaya. Purposely, in Shillong, I had not addressed the meeting. I knew that the people from the minority section, specially Bengalees, were being brutally tortured there. So, would it be right to go to them during election time and then forget about them ? Alongwith the P.M., I had attended eight public meetings in Tripura. I had toured the length and breadth of Tripura with Santoshda. After seeing the spontaneous reaction of the people, I had been convinced that we would win. What I had not known then was that, a deal had aleady been struck. We spoilt our own chances. On minor grounds, the CPI(M)'s demand, for President's Rule was accepted. We lost what had been a sure win for us! A gift of a State Government was made to the CPI(M)! Unable to bear the hurt I had said, "This is a victory for the High Command". Meanwhile, the "call of the struggle' beckoned. The battle call of the bugle could be heard. Fellow workers had been demanding that there should be no deviation from the path of struggle. Programmes were chalked out. Alongwith the demand for reintroduction of teaching of the English language from Class I, establishment new industries, solution to the unemployment problem and building up an impartial administration, there was the necessity for widespread protest against the leftist torture on the people. On behalf of the Youth Congress, the programme for "Writers" buildings blockade' was announced. At first the programme was scheduled to be held on 14th July. Due to the death of Sri Nurul Hasan, Governor, it was postponed to 21st July. I had decided that roads leading to Writers' Buildings would be blocked at five points. I had already been touring the districts, gathering public opinion. I had been holding regular meetings with my colleagues, so that we could work unitedly. There had been immense response from the districts. On the other hand, the Left Front Government was also receiving reports from district administrations that lakhs of people would be joining the programme. To foil this programme, a blueprint was prepared. On 19th, all the DMs and SPs from the districts had been called over to Writers' Buildings. They had been given a confidential circular and instructions had been issued that under no circumstances the people were to be allowed to converge in Calcutta and stern measures should be taken to stop them. The police had been instructed not to allow the entry of any vehicle carrying the participants to Calcutta. The CPI(M) had not realised that we had come to know of this. I remember sitting in a room one evening in Nizam Palace discussing the details of the programme with my co-workers, one of our colleagues had come and told us about this conspiracy. He had been informed by a police officer. At first I could not comprehend how it possible that those who proclaimed to be democratic and progressive could stoop to such a level to choke the voice of a democratic movement. These were the same people who had, in the name of democracy, burnt buses and tramcars, spread the flame of unrest in rural Bengal just to come to power. What a changeover? This was absolute misuse of power. Anyhow, on hearing this, I had contacted the DG (Police) and Chief Secretary. I telephoned and said, "You are aware that this programme is for the benefit of the common man. We have informed you about this through an official letter. There are previous instances of Writers' Buildings blockade. Besides, this will not mean forcible occupation of the Writers' Buildings itself. We will assemble at five points and peacefully demonstrate to show our protest. For what reason and with what authority are you trying to stifle our movement? People travel in buses and trucks to meetings organised by any political party. People don't fly like the birds to attend the CPI(M) meetings. So why are you trying to create trouble? Is it your job to choke our voice of protest so that we may not be able to speak about the problems of the common man?" Both had replied, "Madam, we cannot do anything about it. These are the Government's instructions. We have to obey". I had realised that the conspiracy went deep, and the Cheif Minister was the main conspirator. From the morning of 20th July, our important leaders and workers were put under surveillance. We had spared no effort to ensure that there would be no trouble on 21st July. I had tried a lot so that the Left Front's attitude would tone down. In the end, 21st July was a different story-the strings of the sitar rendering a horrifyingly sorrowful tune, the sound of which I shall carry with me always.

What happened on 21st July? Everything has come out vividly in the newspapers. Though oft repeated, the blood drenched 21st July is still in "my deepest dreams, deeply embedded in my thoughts". At about 11.30 a.m. I had left home and had first gone to Mayo Road crossing. Already, more than a lakh of people had gathered there. I had found the people extremely restless and I asked, "What has happened?" They had told me, a short while ago the Congress leader Pankaj Banerjee had been inhumanly beaten up by the police and had been hit on the head. He had been taken to the hospital. I thought that, as the people were so agitated, the situation could explode. It had to be controlled. I had asked everyone to sit down peacefully. Our meeting was being conducted from a matador, which had flags and the mike fixed on it. I had appealed to the policemen to step back so that there would be room for everyone to sit down. I do not know why the police from the beginning had taken up a different stance that day. They had not paid heed to my request. I had told Sobhanda, "You carry on with the meeting and let it be peaceful. I am going to Brabourne Road, then I shall come back". Pillion-riding on a scooter, I had proceeded towards the Brabourne Road meeting.

When we were approaching Writers' Buildings I had seen Saugatada coming. He had been leading a group of agitated party workers. Saugatada had told me that more than a lakh of people had assembled at Brabourne Road and the police had resorted to lathi-charging and had not spared our leaders also. They had climbed up on the dais and cut off the wire of our mike so that our speeches could not be heard by the general public. I passed by Writers' Buildings and saw an endless ocean of people gathered near Brabourne Road. The police were not allowing even one lorry to enter. At various roads, the workers were being stopped, but can the wave of humanity be stopped in this manner? Some CPI(M) cadres had been waiting on the terrace of a building right across the road. As soon as they saw me approaching, they started throwing bricks. The police had ignored this and charged at our workers with thick wooden sticks and started teargassing. Though the mike had not been working, I had tried to address the gathering. The police had climbed on the dais and hit my head with a rifle butt. Another batch of policemen had started firing teargas shells. Their target had been the dais. Seeing the "killer attitude" of the policemen, my colleagues had forced me down from the dais; I stood near the platform. My hips had started paining unbearably. Hridayananda Gupta, Councillor, had tried to move me away from there. At that point, two teargas shells had come flying and burst at my feet. The police were then ready to start firing. The guns had been pointed at me, ready to go off any moment. I told them, that if killing me would satisfy them, then they could go ahead, but they were not to shoot at innocent people. They had not allowed photographers to come near us, in case the pictures of what was happening were flashed in the newspapers the next day! Seeing the guns pointed at me, my personal security guard Maity Babu had pulled out his own service revolver and yelled, "Things had gone too far. Now I'll be forced to use my gun".

I had noticed a strange thing that day. Normally I do not take any security personnel with me. Yet, from the morning, a team of 5-6 personnel from the Special Branch had been following me in another car. One of them was Mr. Biswas. I saw his spectacles broke when a policeman hit him. Though there had been blood pouring from the cuts on his forehead and brow, it had not seemed to bother him. Can you imagine, even the safety of the person who was there to guard me was in danger! The teargassing had continued. There was smoke everywhere making visibility poor. It had been aching all over my body and I felt like fainting. In that condition, I had somehow reached the traffic stand and sat down on it. A few selected CPI(M) cadre had been given the task of hitting us. Saugatada had been sitting beside me and he was badly hit on the shoulder. The battle between the police and public was on. We were sitting in the midst of it. The police had again charged at us. There were some policewomen just in front of us. They became adament. They virtually revolted and refused to hit us. The policemen left us for the time being and went towards Howrah Bridge. Their female counterparts had literally threatened them. That day, at Brabourne Road, I stood in front of the gun barrel, but I had not allowed people to be killed there. The news came that in Strand Road the crowd was immense and the meeting was going on. In Bowbazar, Sudipda and Bakshi were carrying on with the meeting; there also the crowd had been massive. In Dharmtolla, the crowd had been really huge. Sadhanda, Gaffarda, Gopal, Ujjal and Naresh Chaki were conducting the meeting. The news from Mayo Road was horrifying-the police had fired, killing some people. Immediately I had decided, despite the injuries, somehow I had to reach Mayo Road. For, if the news of Mayo Road killing spread elsewhere, the public would naturally become agitated, the police would again start shooting and a bloodbath would follow. I had felt that if I left, the crowd might move off and they would be spared from being killed in the hands of the monsters.

By then the pain had become unbearable. Somehow I had managed to get inside a car. We had proceeded, in the back I was nearly lying on the laps of my colleagues. At the approach of Mayo Road, I had noticed a police ambassador car. Mayo Road had turned into a battlefield. Continuous shooting and teargassing had been going on, yet, the people had not fled. I wanted to get down, but the police car had tried to lead us elsewhere. Having no other option, Gautam, one of my colleagues, had gripped the steering-wheel and stopped the car. At that point, another police car had come and bashed against this car. The door of our car was flung open and the door of the other car had flown open banging against my body. After that a darkness engulfed me as I lost consciousness.

When I had regained consciousness, I found myself in hospital in the midst of oxygen mask, saline-drips, doctors and nurses. I had not known then how many rounds of bullets had been fired and the number of persons killed. The horrifying details I had learnt later. It had been like the massacre at Tian-An-Men Square. The police CPI(M) combine, the reign of terror, the lathi-charge, the rifles, the pipeguns, the torture over the innocent people all this couldn't be forgiven. The police had fired 500 rounds of bullets approximately. Yet, none of our fellow-workers had left the battlefield.

In Esplanade East, one of our colleagues had been tying the party flag on the dais. The police pointed the gun at him. With the Congress flag held high in his hand he had said, "Shoot, shoot, since you have the gun you can kill, but under Mamatadi's leadership our movement will continue. You may kill us, but you cannot stop our movement". Then the police bullet came and he, with a smile on his face and the call of Vande Mataram on his lips, had accepted death.

That day the police and CPI(M) cadres were reduced to the role of "Man-Eaters". Without any provocation the mounted police had charged at the peaceful gathering of the people. Innumerable persons crying out for water had instead faced the bursting tear-gas shells, the lathi-charge and the firing. I am grateful to the clubs in the Maidan. They had given shelter to the people in distress, water to the thirsty and a lot of co-operation to people facing danger. The heart of Calcutta had witnessed a bloodbath. On the main thoroughfare, the reason of the deaths was evident in the bloodshed. The number of dead and injured had been rising, yet the Chief of Calcutta Police had praised the officers of his force by saying, "Well done". This is what he had told to the journalists. Our fellow workers had been taking the injured, one by one, to the hospitals. In Calcutta alone, two hundred persons were hospitalised; the number in the districts was uncountable. I express my gratitude to those spirited Youth Congress friends, who, in spite of the danger, had not fled leaving the injured and dead behind. Like soldiers, they had lined up to donate blood to save the lives of their fellow workers. They had kept vigil in the hospitals, night after night, extending help, friendship and hope. That day there had been many who had died on the spot; and three or four persons died after being admitted to hospital. Thirteen young men lost their lives in police firing. Even after such a grave incident, the shameless Left-Front Government had not been conscience-stricken, nor had they felt any remorse. They had not even issued a token condolence message and without giving any reason had rejected the demand for a judicial probe. Praise to the Marxist Government! Blessed is your conscience!

Jyotibabu, do you remember the days of the Food Movement? Your protest movement over the death of Nurul in Basirhat in police firing? Do you remember the burning of fourteen tram-cars when you were protesting against the one-paise bus-fare rise? And, today? As the Home Minister, being in power, your beliefs are reversed? That day, enraged at the death of thirteen fellow-workers, the Youth Congress workers could have, like the molten lava coming out from the depth of the Vesuvius destroyed the seat of Bengal's power-the Writers' Buildings. They had not done that.

So Jyotibabu, the besmirched hero of the ritualistic genocide, the selfish monster, you will have to face trial one day. Just as one cannot shield the blaze of the sun with outstretched hands, you cannot extinguish the youth's burning fervour. With the memory of 21st July stained with the blood of their brothers forever alive in their minds, the youth of Bengal will one day give their answer. They will!

The true character of the persons, whom the people of Bengal had twenty years ago placed with such respect on the seat of power, was now revealed. It had become crystal-clear. They say one thing and do another thing. This is their "progressive" outlook! Indifference to Bengal's eroding culture, heritage and state of education, total disregard for human rights, going abroad each year alongwith their families, ostensibly for Bengal's progress but actually for their own benefit-there is no doubt that this is what the people of Bengal have got after twenty years. They can turn a murderer into a saint. With equal ease they can make any pesson a scapegoat. They enjoy themselves throughly after nightfall and misuse power to clip the wings of humanitarianism during daytime. This is the extent of "progressive" work that they do. After being in politics for so many years, I have now perceived what is reality.

I do not know for how long I shall be able to retain my individuality in the midst of this game of mutual benefit in politics. I know what will be the consequence of these revealations. My near ones and I may myself get harmed any moment. I am not afraid. Man's true power lies in his moral strength. This strength I have received from the countless people of Bengal who consider me as one of them. So, with this strength, I shall fight the demonic, heartless force. Instead of compromising with what is wrong, I pledge to take up any risk to reveal the persons hiding behind masks. I have broached this subject to clarify one thing. However much the influential political leaders may misunderstand me, the common man (to whom I shall be forever indebted) will not do so.

In my life, 21st July is a day of horror and mourning. Through self-analysis and with actual facts in my hand, with sincerity I have put across my perceptions of reality which I had felt before 21st July, 1994. Today's words are dedicated to the memory of the immortal martyrs. I know they are lost in eternity; but their souls will constantly ask, "Will there be justice?" There shall be justice. The martyrs of 21st July are dead, but they shall live forever. They were, they are and they shall be. They will live forever through our struggle.

We had demanded justice and we lost 13 of our co-workers. As I move forward, I still hope for and seek that same justice. Inspite of enormous hostilities and erosion in sense of values in politics, I am going ahead, sometimes in protest and at times amidst opposition. I do not know when this journey will end. I sometime wonder, if cultural renaissance had been possible in Bengal, then why cannot there be a revival of value based politics now? Why will the people of Bengal not unite and protest against the pleasure-seeking political leaders in whom they had placed their trust, but who have deprived them of their dues and taken advantage of their simplicity? When shall we stand united against the combined cruelty of the extortioner and the ruler? Why will Bengal's individuality be lost? Will the people who torture, have the last say in Bengal? Or will our unified voice protesting against injustice make the words of protest stronger?

Most of my "realizations" have been bitter. Many will be pleased, if in bitterness, I leave everything and go away. In the quest for truth, if someone like me dreams of doing something for the people, then these perceptions may be of use.

Blood of 21st July-The Future of The New Generation

For a long time I have been thinking of the new generation and their future. If in any state or society, the new generation does not come forward or is obstructed from holding their head high, the general welfare cannot be achieved. Just before stepping into the 21st century, (the century around which the new generation has laid so much hope) I have been repeatedly thinking-what is the future of the new generation? What are their plans? Who will gift them the fresh full bloomed morning?

We are citizens of India. In our country, there are many states and Union Territories. Here, through the coexistence of all castes, creeds, religions and languages a spiritual bridge has been built within us. The basis of this is unity among diversity. Just as each state has its different problems, so also each has it's individuality. It is through this individuality that each is moving towards its own goal. And, what about us in West Bengal?

At each turn, the name of our state, West Bengal will certainly crop up. We seem to have fallen back in every sphere. People pity us. Some think, it is pulling on-it will pull on, and this seems to be our individuality. Neither do we have any plan for the future, nor do we have the dream of changing course. The main idea is to cling on to a "Chair" as long as possible, get invited as a Special Guest to some public ceremonies, be a subject of speculation or debate or by dupe achieve what enclusively serves self interest. This seems to be the sole aim.

Have we ever thought of where we were, where we are moving, where we have reached and where it will end up? No. There is no need to think of all this. That is because the completely election-oriented politics has snatched away from us our human values, our broad-mindedness and even our abillity to think freely under the clear, open sky. We have stepped into the narrow confinement of selfishness where the mind's horizon has not developed, where enthusiasm, intelligence, intellect have all become like the calm ocean, tranquil and silent.

We who feel proud because we are born in Bengal, we who dream of the unification of the two Bengals, we who amaze others by uttering the names of the universal poet Rabindra Nath, the rebel Nazrul and Swami Vivekananda, why don't we feel the same amazement at our own downfall? The people of the other states of India try to move their own state forward, labour hard with all their energy. On the other hand, we try to pull each other down. We feel jealous whenever some good happens to anyone else. We are busy in trying how to malign and belittle a person of ability. How dare we lower the dignity of Mother Bangal to dust? Is it not high time to ponder upon this? Who has given us this right? Will the new generation of Bengal be a prey to deception only? Will they suffer in despair only?

will they count the days after finishing themselves? Amongst them, some will choose to end their own lives, some will simply pass the time by idle gossiping and hiding away from reality, some will turn into gangsters and some will stay away because they feel that they are burdens on their families. Is this what is ordained for our future generations? Is this state of self-ruin a result of our own attitude of negligence and inability? It is imperative to think (at all levels) about the new generation which is waiting for the spring that has not come, with a lot of hope in their hearts. I feel this is very important. When the government which is supposed to play the role of the guardian instead acts in its self interest only, then the future generation will have to take up the challenge and be self-reliant so that they can stand on their own feet.

I have travelled in many states of India. I have observed what steps have been taken up for the new generation. I have gathered some good experiences also. Let me talk about Maharashtra. I had gone with only Rs. 2,00,000/- for the victims of the earthquake. I had casually asked the President of the State Unit there (he was a minister also) about the number of the unemployed in Maharashtra. I had also asked about the projects for the unemployed youth there. I am giving the gist of the reply I had received- The Government of Maharashtra has taken up a new scheme called the Employment Assurance Scheme. The main points of this scheme are-if any young man or woman wants to work for the Panchayat, then the Panchayat is bound to provide the job. In case it is not possible to provide the job, then until it is available, the unemployed youth will be provided with wages. So, in Maharashtra there is literally no unemployment in the rural areas. The Government of Maharashtra has provided opportunities to the new generation to be self-reliant through its new plans and for this the government should be congratulated. Compare our state with this and think. It is a pity that we do not copy the good things of other states.

I have heard that in Tamilnadu, the workers of factories which have closed down, receive allowances and the government looks after the education of their children. In Haryana, the government provides support and opportunities for agriculture, industrialisation and particularly to the women. In Punjab I have personally witnessed the work culture. I have seen how the hard working, enterprising youth have ushered in the Green Revolution with the government's help. There are many such examples.

The general opinion of the people in other states about Bengalees are-Bengalees like to while away their time chatting, they have become lazy, they don't like doing any other job except well paid government ones and private sector jobs, they are not enterprising at all.

It is true that the Bengalee youth is full of life and is very enthusiastic; they are emotional. Chit-chatting is not something new in Bengal. This is a tradition of Bengal. In a place like Delhi, everyone stays by himself. Inter-personal relations are at a very artificial level there. In Delhi, when people sit down to watch TV at 9.00 p.m. after a day's work or go to sleep, The Bengalee youth will be chatting over a cup of tea bothering about that day's incidents. If we say, that this is a bad habit, then what is the alternate way? It is a fact that Bengalees are not heartless and the inter-personal ties are not artificial. Many positive thoughts come out of the discussions and it is these young men who extend their helping hands to people of the locality. This is the way of life in Bengal. Instead of weeding this state of affairs entirely, the new generation can still be guided correctly and utilised positively. The new generation of Bengal has the intellect, intelligence and is deserving. Yet, what will be their future if eligibility is measured by the political affiliations and all eligibility gets tied up amidst red tapism? Besides, inspite of creating the right climate for industrial development, this state has become the playfield of a few well known groups. Here, there is one industry only which is booming-the multi-storied building construction industry. The entire money is going into the coffers of a few whilst thousands of workers are getting laid off and are counting their days amidst pangs of hunger. 30,000 small scale industrial units have closed down. Under the guise of a strike, there are fashion parades at the drop of a hat. Strikes have crippled the state's economy. Loss of working days is the highest here. The workers have been deprived of their legitimate provident fund dues. Whenever people have protested, there has been and there is even today indiscriminate police firing. Sometimes in Mogra, Sometimes in Santipur, at times in Sujapur and in Suri, in Behala and Howrah, in Coochbehar and Kumamrganj, in Tarapur and Ballygunge and Watgunge. Wherever there is people's protest, there is police firing. On 21st July, 1993, the police fired upon the peaceful, democratic protest meeting. On 22nd February, 1993, the police surrounded the meeting ground in Barasat just as in Jallianwalabagh, and fired upon the assembled crowd without any provocation. A political worker like Madhai Haldar (of SUCI) was not spared when he protested-yes, even though he had a red flag in his hand. At the time of writing this book, the latest incident of police firing (at Sealdah) is still fresh in the mind. There are numerous such episodes.

The youths of Bengal have given their blood, they have received bullets when they have raised the voice of protest, but they have not retaliated because they know tolerance and endurance. They have carried the bodies of their near and dear ones to the crematorium. They have said them good bye with tears and unspoken grief. Yet, they have not taken up the path of revenge. This is the youth of Bengal, the new generation. If I do not felicitate them, then my "perceptions & realizations" will be incomplete.

The youth of Bengal is indestructible. Their future cannot be frittered away. Their moral character must be built up by keeping them engaged and for this a deluge of opportunities has to be created. Large-scale planning with the initiative of the public and private sectors is necessary. Training, financial assistance, marketing infrastructure have to be provided also for the youth (in both areas of industry and profitable trade). Proper infrastructure is required so that those who wish to go in for self-employment projects (to become self-reliant) need not run from pillar to post.

As it is, we do not like to venture out too far away from home whereas the youth of other states go to far off places in case of necessity. We cannot think beyond a posting near our home. I know some Bengalees who have established themselves in other states. So, in case it is necessary, one must move to other states for jobs. Or, if certain things are available at a cheaper rate in other states, such products can be brought over to Bengal for trading. Please notice how the people of Bhutan come over to Calcutta with so many kinds of winter garments during the winter season. If the young men of Bengal can bring over wool and woolen clothes from Bhutan, Delhi and Ludhiana and sell those in Calcutta, they will become self-reliant and self-employed. Electrical goods, crockery and cutlery and cooking utensils of the latest style, crash helmets brought from Delhi and sold in Calcutta can be a profitable business.

I appeal to the Youth of Bengal not to keep on waiting for government assistance and not to go on hoping for jobs-such waiting idle and doing nothing will ruin their future. No work should be looked down upon. One should see any work as a goal to be achieved-then the workplace will become a temple. Start with the small jobs, let your dreams for the future be big. If necessary, you must labour hard for 16 to 18 hours day. You will not have the same vigour of youth in your old age, so don't waste time when you can labour hard. Time, once wasted, does not come back, however much may be your regret. I don't want to sermonise, I am speaking from my own experience. One of my brothers drives a taxi. There are many who tell me that this does not look nice. I ask them," Why? After all work in any form is work! Work should not be rejected. The new generation can give a lot to Mother Bengal.

In the past the words "in trade lies wealth" were used to be oft uttered. The Bengalee traders who were the best in their own line of business are nowadays moving out. It is true that there can be profits as well as losses in business. There can be losses in trade due to any calamity. In such cases, the government owned institutions like Life Insurance Corpn. of India, General Insurance Corporation are there to provide the cover. So, there is no need to be afraid. Counting the days and waiting for others to help is also useless. The number of registered unemployed exceeds the 50 lakh mark in West Bengal. The number is increasing by leaps and bounds. Yet, it is nobody's headache.

In Parliament, I had requested the Prime Minister to call all the Chief Ministers at the meeting of the National Development Council to finalise the employment plans for the jobless. The Prime Minister's Rozgar Yojna, Jawahar Rozgar Yojna schemes, have been launched. In these schemes the funds are provided by the Central Government and the State Governments are responsible for the implementation. I know that in this state, it is the political affiliation which counts the most. Inspite of all these hazards, the present generation will have to move forward. The new generation will have to take up the responsibility of restoring the former glory of Bengal. Although our state has wide scope for the tourism industry, this has not been fully developed due to lack of planning. Every year, thousands of people of our state visit Himachal, Dehra Dun, Hardwar, Rajasthan, Goa and South India. The revenue collection of those States are thus being augmented. Employment opportunities are also increasing through the tourism industry. Just look at our state of affairs. Is there the tourism oriented infrastructure, publicity, sincerity in intention on the part of the government? Where is the initiative at the State government level to attract tourists from other states? We can increase our savings through the tourism trade and gain much out of it. The future generation will have to take up the responsibility of this work. Many persons have innovative ideas, and I feel that there is a necessity to utilise these ideas. From years of experience, I can say that the amount spent on individual development is more than that spent for development in a general level. Nowadays, the inclination is towards-firstly, a job, then promotion, thereafter accomodation and then the child's admission to school. I admit that all this is necessary for a family; but if all this is done for one person only and for the other there is nothing, then where has our social system reached? There must be a balance between the two. I have certainly spoken out some bitter truth, but this is not to hurt anyone's feeling. Let us all realize that we need each other.

Between 1972 and 1977, the people of Bengal have seen one generation. Between 1977 and 1994, the people of Bengal are seeing another generation. Some leftists, some rightists. One particular generation used to raise the slogan, "Some will eat, some will not, this cannot be, this cannot be." They have now occupied the seat of power, and this song is sung no more. Instead, they are saying, "Loot and swallow, finish Bengal." Their conscience has been lost in the stormy current of the Bay of Bengal. Their emotions and enthusiasm now centre around "Rosogolla Festivals". Their ideology has taken shelter amidst the multistoried edifice. Their sport ranges from finishing off the greenery to finishing off lives.

Side by side, a new generation has emerged; for some years they have been protesting against the wrongs, deception and neglegence. In future, the responsibility of building the golden Bengal will be theirs. With this pledge and new hope in their heart, many young people, workers, farmers, ladies and children have laid down their lives. They have welcomed death. They have not looked for escape routes in the midst of their protest. They have learnt to conquer fear. In district after district, the number of youth and students who have joined together is like the deluge. They will rise above the narrow confines of politics, the spirit of creativity will drive them on, they will engage themselves to constructive works and the fields of competition and will surely offer themselves at the feet of Mother Bengal. This is my firm belief.

This soil of Bengal is our birthplace. This soil is purer than gold to us. Let the pledge of the new generation be to build a creative work environment and not go for loot and pillage. We shall not see again in their mortal form, the martyrs who have laid down their blood, but their sacrifice which binds the new generation to the responsibility of completing their unfinished task. It is the responsibility of the new generation to give full respect to the martyrs. This is my feeling for the youth who want to offer something for the people's welfare. Those who have given and gone, those who have fought to give, they are the new generation. Deriving my power to sustain and endure from the elders, taking the good wishes of the mothers and sisters as my stregth, I have expressed some of my feelings and realizations.

There are many, without whose help we would have lost our way in the midst of various movements. The number of such persons is large. In this short span I have not been able to mention their names; for this I beg forgiveness. For the new generation I offer my fondness and good wishes-with a happy heart.

It will be an injustice if I do not pay respect to those revered individuals with whose blessings I was able to bring to the people the various movements-right from the Save the Greenery to 21st July. They have sheltered me like the peepul tree and they protect me even today. The inspiraiton that they have given has illuminated our path. What I have received from them from time to time is my life's most incomparable and precious asset.

The poet Subhash Mukhopadhyay, poet Nirendra Nath Chakraborty, respected Gouri Sankar Ghosh, Sanjib (dada), Dwijen Mukhopadhyay, Sabitabrata Dutta and other honourable persons are the selfless personalities whom I have seen in my life.

Apart from this, I am indebted to Mamata Sankar, Prodyut Dutta, Sailen Manna, Prasun Banerjee, Prasanta Banerjee, Naimuddin, Subhas Bhowmick, Jyotsna Dutta, George Baker and a host of others. They have not chased "the rewards of power", but have chosen to be human beings who stand by their fellow in the hour of need.

Experience has enlightened me about reality to a great extent; I shall learn more. From what I have realized till

21.7.93, I am placing here certain thoughts. The inspiration of my "Realizations" is the new generation. It is this generation around which I centre my dreams:-

"I shall return to these shores-to this Bengal,

Perhaps not in the human form;

Perhaps in the form of the white-breasted kite or as a small black bird;

Perhaps I shall come to this land of winter harvest ceremonies as the morning crow;

I shall be borne with the mist amidst the shadows of the jackfruit tree."

I pray with folded hands:

"Still, let me die amidst these fields and shores,

And not where the Krishna and Jamuna flows.

Let the breathe of the waves of this river touch my eyes and face,

Let Beautiful Bengal be alive within my heart."

With the blood-smeared memory of 21st July in our heart, we grieved in silence. Our dear ones were laid to rest and we were completely devastated. Those who had heartlessly taken away the thirteen young lives, did not even offer their sympathies. Instead, they announced in open meetings and before the press that we were responsible for the thirteen deaths. One "knowledgable leader" of the ruling party sarcastically told the newspapers, "Let the families of the martyrs go to Mamata's house and squat in front of her." This is called "the senile mind at the end of the road". That leader had perhaps forgotten about the families of the martyrs (of their agitations) during the fifties and sixties. After twenty years of Leftist rule, they still suffer the agony of hunger, but cannot speak out.

Our protest movement was for the benefit of the people, to speak on their behalf. The youth of Bengal had given the call in their endeavour to make the voice of protest strong. Instead of justice, they received injustice. For this hellish human slaughter (like in the byegone pratice of human sacrifice), "they' did not have a iota of remorse. Under the influence of the "intoxicating fumes of human blood' their "cold-bloodedness" hid behind the portraits of Karl Marx and Lenin and smirked. They had failed to realize that the colour of the blood which flows through every being does not bear the colour of any political party. They had forgotten:

"Above all, comes the truth of mankind

and nothing is more than this."

Not a single member of the martyrs' families went to "them" to beg, because these families have nothing else but abhorrence for "them".

I am grateful to certain respected and well-known personalities. They stood by us in our moment of crisis and extended their hands of blessing and affection. It was they who inspired me to decide (while I was still under medical care) that we would stand by the families of the martyrs with the help of the common men and not seek any help from the government. I made the plans for setting up the Martyrs' Memorial Fund whilst in hospital. The poet Subhash Mukhopadhyay (the very revered person whose habit is to stand by people in danger and distress) became the chairman and a six-member committee was set up with Prasun Banerjee (Arjun awardee) and Prasanta Banerjee as members. During that time I have seen one or two public figures withdrew, either out of fear or in self-interest. Whatever be it, I appealed to the common people of Bengal through newspapers to send their helps by cheque or bank draft to the specified bank within a certain date. I was overwhelmed at the response; they responded wholeheartedly to my appeal, although I was not even a member of the committee. Our target was Rupees One Lakh for each martyr's family-a total of Rupees Thirteen Lakh was needed. With the people's blessings, the figure eventually went up to Rupees Twenty Lakhs. Many cheques and drafts were sent even after the time limit, but we could not accept those because of the usual rules and regulations. So we returned those with grateful acknowledgement.

School children saved from their tiffin money, many housewives saved from their household expenses and donated to the fund. Many service-holders, labourers, members of different trade unions worked overtime and deposited one day's wages with the bank-they had truly honoured the memory of the martyrs.

The committee held a meeting under Subhash Mukhopadhyay's (Gyanpith awardee) chairmanship and decided to give Rupees One Lakh to each family through the Unit Trust Pension Scheme. In this scheme Rupees One Lakh would remain intact and they would receive Rupees 1125/- every month to meet up their needs. Apart from this, each family would be given a cheque for Rs 10,000/-. I remember, the public meeting was in progress on 2nd October, '93 at Hazra crossing (the birth anniversary of Gandhiji). It was raining heavily. Ignoring the inclement weather, at least ten thousand people had assembled. At that time the people of Maharashtra were badly affected by a major earthquake. I told Subhashda, "After giving the money to the martyrs' families, there is still some left over. We can help the people of Maharashtra." Subhashda said, "The idea is good, but since the money was raised from the public, before doing anything with it, it is our duty to take their permission." I made the proposal from the dais. The people gathered, wholeheartedly gave their assent. This is our Bengal-standing by people when they are in trouble. Subhashda announced from the dais, "Mamata, you go on our behalf with the money. Extend your support to the people affected by the earthquake, with this gift of love from the people of Bengal. This will be a morale booster for them." According to Subhashda's instructions, I handed over Rupees Two Lakhs to the Maharashtra Government. Besides this, we handed over to about one hundred persons, who had been injured in the police firing on 21st July, according to the extent of their injuries , amounts ranging from Rs. 3000/-, Rs. 5000/-, Rs. 20,000/- to even Rs. 35,000/-. Even after giving all these, Rs. 95,000/- had remained. On "Condemnation Day', 21st July, '94, at the Sahid Minar Maidan meeting, amounts ranging from Rs. 1000/- to Rs 10,000/- were given to each of the martyrs' families, and Unit Trust Certificates of Rs. 5000/- were made out in their children's names to help them to complete their education. The "audit report" was now over, that is, the entire sum had been properly utilised. The All India Youth Congress had given Rs. 25,000/- to each martyr's family and the AICC had sent through the Pradesh Congress Committee Rs. 30,000/- for each of the families. We had been able to hand over Rs. 1,65,000/- to each of the families. Without the people's blessings, this enormous task would not have been possible. Job had been provided to one member, each from four families, and we shall not rest till the others are similarly provided with employment.

On one side there was the sincere spontaneous response of the people to help the affected families, on the other, the warped jealousy evident in the endless statements issued by some upstart leaders. They had raised the question-how could such a huge amount of money be raised within such a short period? If a person does something to help another, then only can he raise questions. Is it proper for those who had not even contributed a single paise to help the endaugered families, to ask such questions? Before passing any remarks, one must look in the mirror first. We shall live in great happiness, amidst abundance, and the families of those killed while participating in our movement will exist without food and clothing-can this be allowed? If some persons find something evil in this act of helping the bereaved families, then they can go on doing so. If they find it necessary, they can form an enquiry committee and appoint a person of their choice as chairman of it also, but they must remember, "the force of virtuousness even sways with the wind." These persons are progressive in appearance, but inwardly they are mean minded. To argue with them would mean lowering oneself to their lowly level. Though they had kept silent that day, the helpless families will ask them for explanations. Time marched on in its own stride. Again the web of conspiracy was being woven. On behalf of the party in power, Goebbel-like, it was being circulated that our movements are always voilent. Amazing! When we had been demanding compensation for the afflicted people of Behala, who had become paralysed after consuming adulterated oil, the CPI(M) had attacked our procession. I remember the photographs that had appeared in the next day's newspapers-Myself standing alone, confronting the CPI(M) attack, my colleagues having been already beaten and driven away. Have you forgotten the incident of 16th August, '90? Do you remember who had tried to kill me, after having chased away everyone from the scene? Do you remember who had made arrangements so that life-saving oxygen and saline would not be available for me when I was hospitalised after that incident? Remember the behaviour of the policemen towards our women processionists, during our march to Vidhan Sabha in protest against the price-rise-do such things happen in any civilised country? Has there been any trial after the torture on us by inebriate policemen at midnight in Lal Bazar on 7th January, '93?

When a helpless dumb girl, ravished by Soubhagya, a "comrade" of the ruling party, went to Writers' Buildings for justice, she was the victim of unutterable ill-treatment. This is our misfortune. Was there any trial of the policemen who had killed workers who had been demanding their rightful dues, at Mograhat? There had been police-firing in Sainthia, Tarapur, Howrah, Behala, Baguihati, Burdwan, Hariharpara, Kumargunj, Cooch Behar-everywhere innocent people had been killed. Had there been any trial anywhere?

There will be no trial, so that the bigger truth can be suppressed. The plan is to create a diversion. When one jackal calls, the others in the pack also start howling. In the same way, "comrades" in all the districts take up the same refrain. Since Mamata is their common enemy, some friends are also told to join the chorus. So they yell, "Their movements mean trouble always ending in police-firing".

I have organised many movements in my political career since 1970. Apart from the 21st July, '93 and the 22nd February, '94 (Barasat incident), another death by police-firing took place in Behala. Raghunandan Tewary was killed at point-blank range by the police, after we had been arrested and taken away from the spot.

We were not in kumargunj, so why was the student named Partha Singha Ray killed in police-firing. We were not present in Sujapur, where five persons were killed when the police fired. We were not in Sainthia, so why did five persons die when the police fired? Rabin-Biman-Haider of Cooch Behar, Mrs. Bimala De of Howrah, Manas Banerjee of Burdwan, all died in police firing-Why? Had we been there then? Just sometimes back, the police had resorted to firing at Sealdah, in which five persons had died. I had been bed-ridden in hospital then, so why did the police start shooting?

Why had the CPI(M) cadres, dressed-up as policemen, use guns on 21st July? The common man is aware of the reasons. The CPI(M) leaders were having sleepless nights after seeing the tremendous success of our Brigade Parade Ground rally. That is why they had engineered the "riots" following the 6th December incidents. Of course they had pretended to show a lot of concern. They had systematically used well-known anti-social elements for creating the riots, with total disregard for the common man's safety. The leaders of the party in power were also contended, thinking that all our protest movements would stop after the riots. During the riots, I had worked throughout the nights, keeping in touch with the riot-affected people of Tiljala, Tangra, Topsia, Park Circus, Garden Reach and the Administration, not caring for my own safety. I had visited those areas during curfew to restore peace. We thank the people of rural Bengal. Though they had been conscious of things going on, they had shown extreme restraint during the riots. So, after peace was restored, we started going to them to express our gratitude.

It had been decided that the march to Writers' Buildings that had been announced at the Brigade Parade meeting, would take place sometime in March; because of the riots, this was postponed. The speculations were rife. It was being rumoured that we did not have the capacity to carry out such a big protest movement. At that time I had been touring the districts, gettting a feedback of the proposed programme. Everyone had agreed that the movement should be based on five main demands. The CPI(M) Party had thought that it would flop. Inspite of disallowing entry of lorries and trucks carrying the processionists and also intimidating them, news had filtered to the leaders sitting in the air-conditioned rooms of the Writers' Buildings that ten lakh people had already assembled in Calcutta. The ever slumbering emperor was jolted out of his sleep. The order was issued, "They are coming to usurp the chair. Kill them, kill them, fire as many rounds as you can." One thing was crystal clear. The plan was that, some of their 'pet' newspapers would come out with the pre-conceived stories that the police were not to be blamed; they had been ruthlesssly attacked and had to flee! In this context I am mentioning one thing. I believe there is no lack of honest and efficient officers in the police force. They, like us, are somebody's son, brother or husband and maligning them alongwith the others is objectionable-I do have the guts to admit this. However, there are some policemen in the higher echelons, who, to get their children admitted to medical colleges under the CM's quota, to build houses made of exorbitantly priced marbles from Rajasthan, to get out of turn promotions or to amass wealth for their future security, make one-time 'gift' to their masters by obeying their orders to kill.

I decided to do as Lenin had said-'One step forward, two steps backward'. I decided to adopt the policy of retreat and advance. I decided to go to the people's court and listen to their woes. Before doing that I went to Rajasthan and Madhya Pradesh on Pranabda's request. Despite the back injury, which was the 'gifts' of 21st July, I went there to campaign for the Congress Party. By road the journey took thirty-six hours and inspite of the pain, I had gone and interacted with the people. Without pretending otherwise, I can admit that my campaigning had partially contributed to the Congress candidate's win. I went to Mana Camp from Raipur in Madhya Pradesh. For a long time the people of Mana Camp had been requesting me to visit them. Even though it was a one-day visit, I was very pleased to meet the refugee families from erstwhile East Bengal, now rehabilitated there. It was like being back in one of the refugee colonies in Bengal. The Congress candidate for Mana Camp had won, I had liked it. Normally, I do not eat anything while on tour-programmes, but in Mana Camp I had not been able to refuse their sincere requests. I have visited many places, but never have I tasted such food. They had repeatedly requested me to visit them again.

After hearing of the Mana Camp visit, the people of Dandakaranya also requested me to visit them. I was unable to risk the long journey because of my back injury. The Congress candidate there lost by just 300 votes. The Congress MP from Dandakaranya, Arvind Netam still says, "If you had gone there even once, the people would have made up the deficit of 300 votes." I regret not having gone there. I beg forgiveness from the people of Dandakaranya. If I ever get the opportunity, I will definitely go there.

After the Vidhan Sabha elections were over, we resumed our political programmes. Just before that, we had organised the condemnation meeting at Esplanade East on 21st August '93. It had rained heavily the night before. I, with my colleagues had been busy with the preparations. Suddenly, a fellow-worker had come and given us the news that two of our colleagues from Howrah had been seriously injured. They had been hospitalised. He had got the news from the police. The police was passing it off as an intra-party affair. I had shuddered in apprehension. The next day was our programme. I had wondered-who was responsible for this conspiracy, and for what reasons? I had rushed to P. G. Hospital immediately. On reaching there, I had heard the news that Debuda and Utpal both had expired. I know there had been much controversy over this issue, but few people know that we had been on good terms. Not even once had there been any difference of opinion. I had lost thirteen colleagues on 21st July, and within a month, another two were gone. I returned home with a heavy heart.

I rung up Somenda next morning and said, "Whoever is responsible for this, should be punished. Let us jointly condemn this." He had replied, "Not today, I am very sad. We will call a joint press conference later on." However, this did not take place.

Meanwhile, people had started pouring in, so our programme could not be cancelled. Pranabda and Maninder Singh Bitta had already arrived. During the course of the meeting, we bitterly condemned this incident.

Then started the political intrigues. The battle of issuing statements and counter-statements commenced. Each one started accusing the other. Without the benefit of an enquiry, certain "firebrands" started accusing persons.

On that day, I had pledged to put in all out effort in our fight for the Chowringhee bye-elections. That day had also been the starting point of a conspiracy entangling all of us in a web of party intrigues. I still believe that, if there is a proper enquiry, people will know the truth-who had engineered the twin murders, who had manipulated behind the scenes, who had tried to divert people's attention from recalling the bloodstained day of 21st July, and of the attempts those were made to malign certain persons and also the name of the CPI(M) leader who had sheltered the real murderer. However, if the protector becomes the killer, then it is very hard for the true facts to be revealed; but it will swety come out one day. We shall be at peace only when the actual person responsible for this is punished.

The revelations do not end here. The next phase centres on the Chowringhee bye-elections. Bholanath Sen was our unanimous candidate. I started campaigning even though I was dejected and in great pain. As far as possible, I interacted with the people requesting them to vote for Bholada. The people of Chowringhee had always voted for the Congress, so why should they be blamed for what happened?

At that time, the infighting within the Congress Party used to hit the news headlines daily. By any means, the congress candidate had to be defeated. Then only would I be annihilated. Since I was their enemy, why didn't my detractors expel me from the party? Just to take revenge on me, they betrayed a person like Bholanath Sen. For the time being we may be quelled, but I know the real facts and so do the common people. Bholada lost by just 500 votes; 1400 blank votes had been deposited in the ballot boxes! Some of Bholada's agents, to whom he had given responsibility, did not carry out their duties properly for personal gains. The day before the elections, I heard that there would be rigging at the voting centres in St. Xavier's School, La Martiniere School and Collins Lane. I had rung up the Park Street Police Station O.C. Bomkeshbabu and informed him. I had also told the person in charge of Bholada's elections (for those centres). When everyting became crystal clear, I understood the extent of the betrayal. Some businessmen (whom I can name) had joined hands and provided funds for this conspiracy. By ensuring Bholada's defeat, they intended to prove that people had rejected me also. On the one hand the misuse of political power, on the other succumbing to the lure of money-this situation was getting at me. I was mentally devastated and my feelings were deeply hurt. Certain persons submitted electronically typed allegations against me in Delhi saying that I had failed. Today, I do not hesitate to admit that I had not been able to equal the conspiracy that was laid out in battlelines to oppose me. I had been responsible for what would take place outside the booths and not inside them. How was I to understand that a game of mutual benefits would take place inside the booths? I have never learnt to mistrust anyone-this misplaced trust has let me down many times. This, I realised later on. The agony of 21st July and 20th August and the defeat in the Chowringhee bye-elections-I do not know how much patience and self-endurance one must possess to withstand such pain.

I read Swami Vivekananda's 'Call to the Nation'. That gave me inner strength. I decided-I will not stop; I will go forward. In this journey, one should not think of material rewards. Therefore, I pray to God "Hurt me as much as you want. Let my mind be crushed and wrenched with this hurt, but give me the strength to overcome this pain."

Times changed. The beat of drums heralded the Pujas. Making me forget all my pain the Goddess Durga consoled me, "Think afresh, start the journey again; think of whatever is happening in your life as your trial by fire. You must overcome this test." The Durga Puja, Kali Puja and Parliament session were over. Days passed by and my mind underwent a transformation. I hoped again. I decided to start the Jansanjog Yatra on 12th January (Swami Vivekananda's birth anniversary) to get to know the people living in the remote corners of Bengal, far away from Calcutta.

The tour started on 12th January, '94 from Belpahari in Midnapore. The first phase ended on 23rd January (Netaji's birth anniversary). The second phase started on 30th January (Gandhiji's death anniversary) and ended on 12th February. I learnt much during this tour which I would not have done sitting in Calcutta. I was able to get to know the people living in the remotest villages, talk to them and get to know their problems.

Belpahari is situated at the border of Bengal and Orissa. This is primarily a tribal area. I reached Belpahari on 11th Februaty. It was night then. I was accompanied by three legislators, Saugatada, Sadhanda and Sovanda and some Youth Congress leaders. I had told the local leader Subratada, "I want to start the tour from a tribal village, tomorrow." I wanted to see how the people lived and whether they had received any government aid. There was a village, two kilometres away, entirely surrounded by jungles. It was unapproachable by car. I decided to go by scooter and then on foot. The police did not know where we were heading for; they started following us. We tricked them and they were left behind. We reached Joygrám. I went from hut to hut and met nearly all the families. I asked if they had received any government aid. They had not even heard of such a thing, let alone receive it. Noticing a man sitting on a verandah eating something, I had asked, "What are you eating?" The reply was, "For eleven months in a year we do not get rice to eat, so we get roots and ants (yes, ants) from the jungles, dry them and then cook them to make a concoction. We eat that concoction." I noticed many of them had sores all over their bodies. I asked what they were and how they had got them. They replied, "Haven't you understood? When we go to the jungle to catch the ants, they attack us. The sores are from their bites." I was astounded. Our 'brave' government worries much about Kalahandi (Orissa), but does not think about the plight of these people. There are still people in Bengal existing on roots and ants. As a proof we video-taped everything. Afterwards I heard that the DM had gone there and threatened the people for having told the truth to us. Now I have seen with my own eyes the vast disparity-one section of people immersed in wealth and another section living in the backwaters, existing on ants and roots, totally unaware that they are eligible for government help. One day if the latter demand an answer from the so-called upper class, will it be wrong if they do so?

May be after I came away the Administration had woken up, but one question remains unanswered. There are numerous schemes like Indira Abashik Programme, Jawahar Rozgar Yojna, IRDP, NREP and RLEGP for the welfare of the tribals for which the Central Government gives money. Why have these people been denied benefit of these opportunities? Can they not hope for the barest minimum of sympathy from the State Government? After coming back, I had informed the Minister of Welfare of the details. The same conditions may be existing in many farflung villages of Bankura, Purulia and Midnapore for which there are no government or non-government statistical details. Only if a private investigatiion is conducted, the truth will be revealed.

From Joygram we went back to Belpahari. There the tribal people joined the meeting. With the beating of drums they expressed their sincere welcome. There was a sea of people lining the route from Belpahari to Seelda. From school children to housewives and the elder generation, all were waiting eagerly for the meeting to start. I addressed the meeting. The tribal people of Jhargram sub-division have a long-standing demand. They want all the tribal welfare projects (for that area) to be undertaken by an elected, autonomous organisation comprising of their representatives. Giving due importance to the people's demand, I expressed my support. From Seelda we went to Binpur. I was told that some persons, with the support of the ruling party were running a parallel administration. The people were so tortured that they were frightened to speak up. Murders were common-place occurrences. If they protested or opposed, they were totally ruined, even killed. I came to know of these conditions from the people.

I proceeded towards Jhargram. As we were approaching, we found a ocean of humanity waiting, the huge crowd forcing the wheels of the car to slow down. They were waiting to attend the meeting and make it a success. Normally a fifteen minute's stretch, it took us one and half hours to cross it. We finally reached the Rajbari Ground, the venue of the meeting. With warmth and sincerity, the tribal girls greeted us. I pushed my way through the crowd and somehow managed to get up on the dais. The place was so packed up with people that not 'even a grain of rice' would have found place. The meeting was a great success. After travelling for miles, on reaching Jhargram I had drunk just a cup of tea. From there we went to Rohini. The road to Rohini was bad and difficult to traverse. From there we went to Kesiyari. The people here are constantly tortured by th CPI(M). The meeting was supposed to start at 6.00 p.m. but because of the crowd lining the roads, we could reach only at 11 p. m. Though we were late not even one person had left the meeting ground. I had felt ashamed for not having reached on time. I had been astounded at the patience displayed by the people. In that tour though we had sometimes reached meeting spots at 1.00 p.m. or even 2 p.m., the people had always waited for us and a single person had not gone away. They had always blessed us.

We went to Gorbeta, Chandrakona, Shalbani, Mahisadal, Nandigram, North Contai, Egra, Khejure, Mugberia, Bhagwanpur, Potashpur and finally Pingla. Here the torture on the people by hoodlums belonging to the ruling party had exceeded all bounds. The represed people lining both sides of the roads told us about the torture. I went around, looking for the true picture. We had a jeep with us. We were proceeding towards the meeting ground. Over the loudspeaker (tied on the jeep) patriotic songs, sung in praise of Bengal could be heard. I noticed that over a lakh of people were enthusiastically moving along with us. And, ringing in their minds were the words, "Even after hearing the despair of the countless from both the sides..." There was a huge gathering at Mogra. On our way to Kolaghat, I addressed more meetings. The next day the meetings were at Debra, Kharagpur, Belda, Narayanpur, Nandanpur, Ghatal and Chandrakona. It is necesssary to add something here. The district leaders had arranged for many unscheduled meetings. That is why I could not reach all the meetings on time. In fact, I could not reach some of the spots even. I have never failed to keep an appointment before this, in my political career. In case I get tied up with some special work, I usually inform the organisers beforehand, so that they can reschedule the meeting. I have always disliked not being able to keep my word and I dislike most those persons who mislead people by announcing that I would be present at the meeting. Sometimes I am forced to attend impromptu meetings enroute, whilst thousands are kept waiting at the scheduled meeting ground. This cannot be tolerated. There are numerous such instances. I will tell about an incident that happened in Midnapur-Jalchok is one of the furthest points within Debra Assembly segment. While travelling by road to Jalchok one has to cross a small river. That day, all the meetings were over by 11 p.m. I was thinking-Now I should take some rest. While we were nearing Kolaghat, I came to know that the District Youth Congress President had arranged for an unscheduled meeting. I lost my temper and reprimanded him. Then I felt very dejected. After all, the people did not have any fault-how were they to know that the meeting had been arranged without my knowledge? Later on, I heard that message had been sent through the police that I was ill and the meeting had been cancelled because of that. I resolved, come what might, I would go. When I reached Jalchok, I found the organisers completely dejected. I explained the actual situation to them. The agitated crowd was hunting for the District Youth Congress President. To avoid detection, he had covered his face and was explaining to the people that the President had not come! People could not be able to recognise him. That only saved the person. I unveiled statues of Indiraji and Rajivji and held a small meeting. The people were pleased. I gave them word that I would come again soon.

I was in Midnapur for six days addressing meetings. From there I went to Kamarpukur which is the birthplace of Sri Ramkrishna. It is considered as a place of pilgrimage. In Hooghly district, our programme started from Goghat, a place where the maximum number of atrocities had taken place. Here the CPI(M) obstructs other political parties from holding meetings. The people feel unsafe. The CPI(M) keeps watch on who is attending Congress meetings and afterwards retaliates by torturing. The aim of my programme was to give them courage to protest against such atrocities. So I addressed meetings at Goghat, Arambagh, Khanakul, Jangipara, Singur, Chanditola and then entered Howrah. On the way I went to Phurphura Sarif in Hooghly district. The Imam Sahib had taken me to his residence. As a sign of respect, I had touched his feet. I met the families belonging to the minority community. They had blessed me. I was pleased that I had been able to visit Phurphura Sarif.

Then I reached Howrah. After addrersing meetings at Borgachia, Khejuti, Bagnan, Shyampur, Andul, Dasnagar, Kadamtola, Amta and other places, I entered Calcutta via

Burrabazar. It was 23rd January, '94. I passed through many streets of north Calcutta and finally reached the five-points crossing at Shyambazar. A meeting was held amidst a huge crowd. I garlanded the statue of Netaji and ended the first phase of the tour.

During the entire tour, we had received the support of the people. Wherever we had gone, we had seen the flood of humanity waiting for us. We had received their sincere co-operation and support. Alongwith the Congress supporters, left-minded people had also joined the meetings and blessed us. On our way from Kolaghat, we were stopped at one point by a large group of people. They said, "Didi, we are the CPI(M) members of the panchyat but in the next election we shall vote for you." I had thanked them. Since I would not be standing for election from that place, what they had meant was that they would be voting for the Congress candidate.

There are still people with conscience, who place human values first and are not bothered with what is Left and what is Right. Their sense of humanism will definitely change the present inhuman conditions. The time for the change is imminent. The change in the social structure comes with a sudden jolt. Nobody can say how and in what form it will come. Nobody can prevent the change. Just as the blaze of the sun cannot be blotted out with two outstretched hands, the wind of political and social change cannot be stopped by anyone. This is what I had perceived during the first phase of the tour.

The second phase of the tour started from North Bengal. North Bengal has always been neglected. I have often heard people from North Bengal say that leaders staying in Calcutta are indifferent to their plight. On 28th January, '94 I boarded the Darjeeling Mail at Calcutta and reached Siliguri the next day. From Siliguri we commenced our tour. Excepting a few blocks, we covered the entire area, from the borders of Siliguri-Jalpaiguri to Dhupguri and Alipurdooar. The entire route was thickly crowded and conceding to the people's wishes we had to hold many meetings. This had made me worried-when would we reach Alipurdooar? The people would be waiting for us there. When we finally reached Alipurdooar, it appeared as if the whole town had come out. Mridul, Bablu, panchayat members, municipal commissioners and other leaders were all present. More than three lakh people-ranging from children to tea-garden workers had come to the meeting. A year ago, many of them had been totally ruined by the devastating flood that had occurred; but the hungry jaws of nature had not been able to diminish their enthusiasm and spirit. They are the people who will one day usher in the new dawn. These people will then chant, "They do not allow us to sing." Who are "they"? They are the persons who had deceived the people and had taught them to sing this very song eighteen years ago. May be, they have not still realised that the words of the song will become a boomerang on them in the future. When they will realise it, it shall be too late. The avalanche has already started. The oppressed common man, whatever party affiliation he may have, remains neglected.

From Alipurdooar we left for Coochbehar. On our way through Jalpaiguri, I addressed many meetings. We reached Coochbehar at night fall. Next day, before starting on our journey, I garlanded Gandhiji's statue. We started on foot from this point. Wherever we went, from Toofangunj,Dinhata, Mekhligunj, Mathabhanga, Tinbigha to Changrabandha, lakhs of people greeted us. I listened to their problems. The farmers left tilling to participate in our meeting.

The labourers left their work to join us. With humbleness, we had accepted their spontaneous and sincere blessings.

"O, Soil of our land, we touch Thee."

Sometimes, en route the children stopped our car. I have a habit of carrying with me sweets for children; I gave those to them. Children do not know anything about politics, they just want to be loved. The sweets, which were a token of my love for the children, pleased them. I felt happy when I saw them, with the packets of sweets in their hands, lining the streets. Since it was winter then, I had carried with me woollen wraps (chadars) for the poor people. Wherever I had seen people not wearing any warm clothes (the poor people of course) I had given them those regardless of their party affiliations. Normally the common people in the villages are simple-minded. They do not understand the cunning intricacies of politics. Certain persons wear the mantle of political ideology, but vitiate the state of affairs in the villages for their selfish ends. The friendly atmosphere of the villages is a thing of the past. Now, on the simplest of pretext, people kill each other and fight among themselves. However, this can still be changed, if narrow- minded political influence is eradicated. Then only can be works get done.

I had always longed to visit Tinbigha, but I had not gone till then because I was not able to accept certain things-I hate betraying people. While I was in Mekhligunj I suddenly decided to visit Tinbigha on my way to Kuchlibari. During the course of the journey, I often stopped and spoke to the waiting crowd and listened to them. The wife and mother of the person who had laid down his life during the Tinbigha movement stood beside me, in front of the martyrs' column and wept inconsolably. I did not have enough words of comfort for them. Later, I had tried my best to help that family. I went to the 'Tinbigha Corridor' and placed flowers at the martyrs' column. I spoke to the

Indian soldiers stationed there. There was crowd standing in the adjoining Bagladesh Corridor. After taking permission from the Bangladeshi soldiers, we exchanged civilities with the people there. As a gesture of goodwill, we placed our chadars (wrap) across their shoulders. They said, "We have heard a lot about you; when we got the news that you are coming, we have come over". All of them repeatedly asked us to visit Bangladesh. After this we started for Kuchlibari. The people there welcomed us with sincere warmth. On our way to Changrabandha, we were stopped by some needy people. They said, "Didi, we are very poor, will you give us some woollen chadars (wraps)?" I gave them all the woollen wraps we had with us. Suddenly I noticed a lone blind man, standing in a corner, waiting with the hope of getting a chadar. Since there was at left any I gave the one I was wearing. From Changrabandha we went to Siliguri. We held a meeting there. The second phase of our tour ended.

The third phase of the tour started on 8th February. We held several meetings in places adjoining Siliguri. From there we proceeded towards Naxalbari. Seeing a roadside teashop we stoped. The shop was run by some tribal youth. While drinking tea, I chatted with them. By then a crowd had gathered. Fearing that the small shop would break in the crush, I quickly left. By then the road to Naxalbari was already crowded-school children, teachers and others-all standing in lines in a quite disciplined manner. I got down at many points and spoke with the children. We got late in reaching Naxalbari. Under the leadership of Tapan Sinha, thousands of people had assembled. After exchanging civilities with them, we proceeded towards Phansideowa. From there we went to Islampur. With us were Karim Chowdhuri, Prasanta Nandy, Tapan Bhattacharjee (a long time colleague), Mihir, Tilak and many others. The next day, we started from Dhalkhola. Haji Sajjad Sahib is the legislator of that constituency. It had started raining so heavily during the night that there were chances of the meeting getting cancelled. The organisers were worried. I decided that even if tthe rain continued, he meeting would be held, and it really did take place. The clouds slowly passed away-might be it was the people's sincere will that made it. Then I went round the entire town of Raigunj. I went to the house of Kamalesh Sarkar, killed in Kumargunj, and met his widow. The Raigunj Municipal Chairman, Mohit Sengupta was with us. We proceeded towards Itahaar. Shamsuddin, Amal and others had organised the meeting. It was a mammoth meeting. From there we continued towards Balurghat. We were supposed to spend the night at Gangarampur. When we reached Gangarampur at 2.00 a.m., we found that the administration was not co-operating There was no accomodation for us. Having no other option, we returned to Raigunj. We went to Tilak's residence. By then it was 5.00 a.m. The previous day, I had addressed numerous meetings. We had not taken any time off for food and rest. We were totally exhausted. It was 'Raigunj Bandh' that day, but I had to reach Balurghat. I was scheduled to go to Partha Singha Roy's house, a student who had been killed in police firing at Kumargunj. Without delay, I proceeded towards his house.

In Kumargunj I had demanded two things-the guilty policemen were to be punished and the students who had been arrested for protesting aginst the killing of a teacher were to be released immediately. I announced that if the demands were not met, I would return on the 10th.

On 9th August, after the meetings at Malda and Buniyaadpur, we took the road towards Balurghat. We were to stay at Hili. Many freedom fighters stay at Hili and

Balurghat. We were to felicitate them. The Congress leader Biplab Mitra was travelling with us. I asked him whether the arrested students had been released. He answered in the negative, saying that it was government intervention that was preventing their release. Suddenly I thought of a plan. The BJP had called for a Bangla Bandh (general strike) the next day. I told Biplabda, "You are a lawyer and you have participated in many protest movements. Can you tell me whether it is correct to detain students when their exams are on? Is there any experienced advocate who will take this case up?" Biplabda named Shyambabu. It was 11 p.m. I told Biplabda, "Let us go to his house." He exclaimed, "At this time of night!" By then I had decided to settle everything that very night. I sent my companions with the District Youth President, Nanda Gopal Roy, to Hili. Just five of us-Biplab Mitra, Biplabda, Sonali, Mukul and I went to Shyambabu's residence. We found the doors closed. One of Biplabda's colleagues scaled the walls, went inside and informed Shyambabu. I am grateful to Shyambabu for welcoming us at that time of night. I told him, "Tomorrow, the bail petitions for the arrested students must be moved in the court". Shyambabu replied, "Tomorrow is the BJP sponsored Bandh. The Administration will take advantage of this and keep the court closed". I told him, "Leave that to us". He told me that Subhash, another advocate had to be informed, because he had already moved a Special Petition regarding this in the court. Subhash came and we all sat together and chalked out the plan. I left and reached Hili at 2.00 a.m. I told Mithu, the Panchayat pradhan, to prepone the programme (meant for felicitating the freedom fighters) by two hours. Reluctantly the organisers agreed. I had to reach Balurghat by 10.00 a.m.. I had already told Subhash that I would be appearing in the court as an advocate alongwith them, and had asked him to keep a lawyer's gown for me, Next morning, Subhash arrived with the gown and we proceeded towards Balurghat court. The administration had no knowledge of our plan; they had not understood what was in store! Just before reaching the court I put on the gown. Then I saw that some members of the ruling party were standing (with the BJP banner) at the entrance. The gate was closed. Before I had got out of the car, the public forced open the gate! I went inside the court, but all the doors of the rooms were closed; nobody was opening them! We were now desperate-we would have to "move". I waited for nearly an hour and pleaded with the judge for opening the courtroom. A few thousand people were present at the time within the court area. Then a message came from the judge-if all the people moved out, then he would come. When this was announced to the people, they moved out. The authorities now started to act because they knew shortly thereafter over one lakh people would assemble at Balurghat. They did not have the power to stop that kind of emotionally charged wave of humanity. At first it had seemed that the court would not open without the permission of the High Court or Writers' Buildings! I was amazed to see how the detractors of the BJP openly supported the same BJP's call for a Bandh in their bid to stop us from getting the students released. Things however did not work as they had planned.

We moved the matter in court. Shankarda led the team; Subhash and Biplabda and other lawyers were also with us. The students were released on bail. I went to the public meeting in a happy state of mind. Nearly three lakh people were present. Seeing the size of the crowd, the authorities were shaken. They were worried-in case such a huge number of people rebelled, what would happen? Our stand was clear. The meeting would proceed peacefully as long as the punishment of the guilty was not announced. Shortly afterwards, a message came. The higher officials wanted to come to our dais to make an announcement regarding the punishment of the guilty. I announced this to the crowd and appealed to them to stay calm. The people responded to this appeal and the officials announced from our dais that those who were guilty of firing would be punished and over a lakh of people who had participated in the "civil disobedience' that day were to be considered as "arrested" and then "released". The demands of the people of Balurghat and Kumargunj and ours had been met by the Administration. I concluded the meeting.

Originally I had told the people that if they wanted justice, they should assemble at noon, then the administration would face their doom! Leave alone Balurghat and Kumargunj, the people of entire South Dinajpur proved how valuable united effort is in any fight against wrong.

The dirty game of politics did not end here. The State Government ordered the Special Branch to find out whether I was eligible to appear as an advocate and whether my name had been enrolled as an advocate in the High Court. Others were adding fuel to the allegations, but they did not know that my name had been enrolled in 1985. I sent a photocopy to the Govt. of West Bengal as a consolation prize! Actually the CPI(M) was shaken by the response of the people and the huge crowd which assembled during the tour. Even after covering 12000 km., everything was working peacefully-this was not acceptable to them. So, the conspiracies started-how to put me in a spot.

From Balurghat I went to Malda. Our public meeting was scheduled to start at 1.00 p.m. Knowing this, the CP(I)M arranged for a meeting just next to ours at 1.00 p.m. Our workers were naturally agitated. I told the Administration-"Okey, let them hold their meeting from 1 p.m. to 3.00 p.m.. After they finish we shall start our meeting." I gave them an extra 1½A hours and then went to the meeting grounds. The CP(I)M had thought, since our meeting was after theirs, the public would feel scared and not come to our meeting. On the contrary, 50,000 people had attended our meeting. Umadi presided. After all the speakers finished I got up to address the crowd. I had hardly spoken for 10 minutes when we heard the shout "gunshots, gunshots:" the crowd ran helter, skelter. Some took shelter under the dais. Later on I came to know that a piece of kerosene soaked cloth had been tied to a cow's tail and set on fire. Then the cow had been let loose amongst the crowd. This was done to disrupt our meeting. The shout-gunshots, gunshots by just four or five boys had been preplanned. It was to scare away the crowd from the grounds. I appealed to everyone to stay calm and resumed speaking. The people who had left, returned to the meeting. At the end, when I was about to raise the slogans, I heard people arguing on the dais. I reprimanded Krishnendu (Malda Youth Congress District President), Balu, Alok and Sonali. They said "Please get up on the car first." From them I came to know of a deep conspiracy.

When the disruptions had happened many people had taken shelter on the dais. Taking advantage of this, a youth, with a revolver hidden on his waist had come up and stood near me, I have been attacked on many occasions. That is why my colleagues are naturally alert. Sonali's suspicions were aroused. She asked the District level leaders whether the youth belonged to our party. On hearing their negative reply, she had asked him to leave the place. When he refused to comply, Sonali had tackled him. Whilst frocibly removing him Sonali had felt the revolver on his waist. Fearing that my speech would get disrupted she had quickly pulled him down. Then he was dragged away by a group of boys. After this incident became known, a report was made to the Malda PS.

Anyway, after finishing the meeting at Malda I returned to Calcutta by Gour Express. The third leg of the journey was over.

One day some people came to me from Sashon (under Barasat PS). Earlier I had heard of what had happened to them. They had been quite well-off-they had a happy family-life, a fishery and landed properties. A CP(I)M henchman (party executioner) had made them penniless. At one time this family used to donate to others-now they were reduced to begging. On some days they would be half-fed, on other days they would starve. Just to test them I had once told them, "You are suffering so much-why don't you go for a compromise and save yourselves." Their reply had amazed me-"No Didi. We shall beg, but not bow down to any gangster. There is no happiness left for us, we are unable to send our children to school, we are fighting with our backs to the wall. So there is no question of compromise. If at all we can go back one day, it shall be with head held high."

Some years back when Siddhartha Sankar Ray had tried to go to Sashon he was not allowed to enter the place. He was surrounded and gheraoed for four hours in front of the police at the instructions of the same gangster. I, too, had gone to Sashon once, and a local "general strike' had been called so that the people would not be able to come to my meeting. They had been threatened that if they came to my meeting they would be killed. I have heard from the people that the law of the land does not work at Sashon-the gangsters' word is law. If anyone wants to visit their relative staying at Sashon, they have to pass through four 'check-points' and give a lot of explanations. In case the gangsters suspect that the visitor belongs to any other political party (that is, not CP(I)M, he is immediately killed and buried. The police know, but they do not keep any record. After all, they prosper from th gangsterism and extortion. What about the Administration? One particular minister controls everything. His orders are like God's command-nobody has the guts to disobey, because obedience means promotions, admission to medical colleges through Chief Minister's quota, 'extra income' and gifts. Will harassed and oppressed people go to such an Administration for justice? Who will look after these people? A 9 year old girl was raped and murdered in this area. Have the guilty been punished? I had informed the Governor, Nurul Hassan (Late) about the lawlessness in Sashon. There was no result. So many incidents have happened in Sashon but the bloodthirsty Administration has not taken any steps. Seeing all this, I decided to organise a Civil Disobedience programme at Barasat on 22nd February '94. We would demand that the people who had been forced to leave Sashon must be reinstated.

The 24 Parganas (N) Youth Congress had given the call for the programme. The District President, Sree Gopal Mukherjee, made extensive preparations (including wall-writings, postering, processions). Such Civil Disobedience programme had been organised in the districts before. We knew that it was impossible for the district administration to keep such large numbers under arrest due to the lack of infrastructure. The usual convention followed is that the authorities come to the dais and announce that such and such number of people had been arrested there and were being released. The number is assessed by seeing the size of the crowd. The authorities had erected a dais besides our's for this purpose. Then why did all the violence happen at Barasat on 22nd February?

After Balurghat, another civil disobedience programme was organised at Howrah. Huge crowds had gathered during the extensive mass contact tour (Jan Sanjog Yatra).

All the meetings were peaceful. The Great Leader of the ruling party realized that if things went on in this way, his party would be washed out from all corners. Then, what would be left! Hence, Hitler's modus operandi was resorted to. The blueprint of conspiracy was prepared inside the airconditioned rooms of Writers' Buildings. Some yesmen of the Great Government were also involved. A meeting was held at Writers' Buildings a few days prior to our programme at Barasat. Two days before our programme I came to know of the plans. A new henchman had been posted as the SDPO. The electric wires of the public address system would be disconnected and hirelings would throw stones from the fringes of the meeting ground at the crowd. Then trouble would break out and the authorities would announce that we had engineered the whole thing. This was the gist of the conspiracy. One must applaud 'Cleverness'. If necessary the "highest bravery" award can be given to those who had prepared the blueprint!

As soon as I came to know of the plan, I informed the Special Branch and Intelligence Branch. I also mentioned a few names to persons who were close to the government, so that the conspiracy did not lead to a dangerous situation. I requested them to take necessary steps. The authorities assured us, "No, No, there will be no trouble. We will announce the number of people who join in the civil disobedience movement and then say they were released." Purposely, I went to the meeting behind schedule. Before this, the MLAs and youth congress leaders had started the meeting. The ground was filled to capacity. My address to the crowd would be followed by the symbolic civil disobedience. I thought, "What if any trouble breaks out during that time? Let the police make the announcement about the arrest-then I will speak." So I told the authorities over the loudspeakers to make the announcement within five mimutes. Contrary to the usual practice I raised slogans instead of speaking first, to enable the police to make the announcement. I saw that the police were not making any move. I told the MLAs to go and talk to the authorities and started to address the crowd. I spoke for 55 minutes; then I saw the police were taking up 'positions'. I realised that orders had come from the 'king' and something was about to happen. So I told the MLAs, "Go and court arrest. We will follow peacefully". The police spread themselves out, in the crowd, without announcing the arrests-things were moving according to the plan I had got to know of earlier. On one hand were the unarmed people and a narrow exit; on the other side were the frenzied violence and torture by 5000 policemen. I was telling everyone not be get agitated when the henchman (SDPO) disconnected the electric wires of the microphone so that my appeal would not be heard by the people. I am not divulging the name of that shameless henchman in case some scrupulous persons bearing the same name are conscience-stricken, although they themselves are innocent. He signalled to the hoodlums who were waiting at the rear of the meeting ground and they started throwing bricks at our dais. Our supporters would never throw bricks at us. Then who threw the bricks? My personal bodyguard broke his shoulder-blade while trying to save me from being hit by the bricks. Sonali, Bani and Tama shielded my head with chairs held high in their hands. I told everyone to go away; but they did not budge and inch. Tama risked his life and brought a ladder and they literally forced me to climb down from the dais. Probably I would have been killed by the henchman if I had not climbed down. By then the CP(I)M cadres (disguised as policemen) were seething. Their task is to annihilate the new generation. The people of Barasat were their prey. They had also charged into a house where a marriage was taking place and did not even spare the bride. She fainted. They continued their torture on schoolgirls. At the risk of our lives, We went towards the hospital. Our workers were bringing the injured. I saw that the policemen were on the rampage inside the hospital complex also. The condition of ten persons was serious. It was necessary to sent them to Calcutta immediately. That day, the hospital superintendent, doctors, nurses and all staff members had extended their kindness and help. I sent the seriously injured persons to various hospitals of Calcutta by car. I arranged for the medical treatment and ambulances. After this, while returning to the superintendent's office. I heard the sound of gunfire inside the hospital. The frightened patients were trying to run away. Five or six persons were hit by bullets. Panic-stricken, I told the superintendent, "Please go and tell the police to stop firing. In any other civilised country has there been such shooting inside the hospital. They do not know what they are doing." At that point a youngman with bullet injuries stumbled into the room. He died in front of us. His name-Gobindo Banerjee. There were some who had not gone to the meeting; they had come to the hospital to find out what had happened. He was one of them. He was killed at the place where people are supposed to be nursed when they fall ill! Such is fate! His family did not even know that the dead body of their dear one was lying in the hospital. Seeing this death, right in front of us, we were at a loss-we did not know what to do. I told the doctors and nurses, "Please go and request the police with folded hands-they are murdering completely helpless people-tell them to stop firing."

I must acknowledge the resoluteness of the doctors and nurses. They literally ordered the policemen to stop firing inside the hospital. After this, the situation calmed down a bit. From railway passengers to shopkeepers, everyone was harassed by the police. They had planned to commit more murders that night. Seeing the situaition, I decided to stay at the hospital that night. The SP threatened the District President of the Youth Congress, "I will kill you". From Barasat I informed the Union Minister of Home Affairs about everything over the telephone. I had no other option. Information came that 100 persons were missing. Many had been dragged into the police vans and beaten up. As the hours went by, the size of the anxious crowd inside the hospital increased. Everyone was searching for their friends and relatives. Inspite of repeated requests there was no clear reply from the authorities about the missing persons. We sent people to several police stations, but there was no information. Around 2.00 a.m. I saw that one honest police officer had arrived. He was truly a gentleman. I learnt from him that out of the 100 missing persons 40-50 persons were in the police station. There was no news of the others. The people were becoming more and more anxious. Pranabda had come to Calcutta from Delhi that night. So I rang him up and requested him to come to Barasat. He reached to us the same night. He had brought some money for medical treatment. This was of immense help.

Even then we did not know the identity of the dead person. Some said he was from Badurai, others said he was from Gaighata. We asked the people known to us to identify the dead body; actually he was from the neighbourhood but nobody could recognise him. I asked one person to find out whether he was wearing anything by which he could be identified. Somebody brought a silver chain with a locket which had been around the neck of the dead youngman. At that point some boys from the neighbourhood came and informed us, "Gobindo has not returned home". Then I showed them the chain and locket. They identified the dead person immediately. I told them not to give the sad news to the family just then. I thought "Let the family members at least sleep during the night. I will go to their house in the morning". After spending the entire night in the hospital I went to Gobinda's house in the morning and broke the sad news. I came to know that Gobindo's wife and three daughters stayed there. They had been staying in Behala previously but had shifted to Barasat to escape from the torture of the CP(I)M. Cruel destiny! I spoke to the grieving wife and children. I did not have adequate words to console them-they had lost their near one. I thought, "They are weeping, let them weep. The tears will less on the burden of their grief." News of the death was sent to their relatives and friends, so that they would come to Barasat. I sent a colleague's car to Gobindo's in-laws house. By early morning I had had a discussion with his brother and brother-in-law. At that time my main worry was how to save the family. Gobindo had been a member of a trade union headed by Shovanda (legislator). Shovanda had been with us throughout the night. It was decided that Shovanda would arrange for a job for the widow within a month. It was arranged and she is now working. We requested the All India Youth Congress President, Mr. Bitta for help and received Rs. 20000/- for each child. This has been invested as fixed deposits for each child. After the post-mortem, the family was sent to their residence in Behala. Gobindo was cremated at Keoratala.

Before leaving Barasat next morning with Gobindo's widow and children, I went to Barasat court. We had came to know that some of the seriously injured persons had also been kept under arrest. They had not been given any medical attention-in fact they were denied drinking water facilities also. Women who had been arrested had not been provided toilet facilities. I do not know whether this information had reached the ears of the Home Minister of the 'progressive' government. These facts have been recorded in the Court. When I went to the court, thousands of people were present.

I requested the lawyers of Barasat court and Priyada to appear in the court lest the crowd should become agitated after my departure. All the persons who had been arrested were released on bail. The police had not kept any record of the arrest of the nine women and had no answer for our lawyers' arguments. Ultimately, truth triumphed. I stayed at Barasat for two days, pacifying the people and returned to Calcutta to attend Gobindo's funeral. Exactly one month later, the state Congress and Youth Congress jointly organised a Condemnation Rally at Barasat.

It was openly circulated after the 21st July '93 and Barasat incidents that "Mamata's movements" meant shooting and trouble. This was being said to prevent us from organising protestmovements for the good of the people. There can be only one comment for such extortioners who are squeezing the people dry-"You are the almightly monarch, so you have become a saint today, and, I, the thief!"

Who are the helmsmen guiding politics today? They who equate ethics with corruption, who are ideologically bankrupt and whose politics do not have any sense of values. Those who used to sing at one time, "They do not allow us to sing our song," are today muzzling the voice of the people by show of force and money power. Before the elections they pretend; their real character is exposed after the elections. Each seems to have descended from the heavens as actors playing different roles. They cannot make any sacrifice-they only know to enjoy life.

In this way attempts are being made to choke the voice of the people. On the one hand the crocodile tears, on the other the politician-mafia-administration nexus. Who will get which tender, who will get the contract for construction of the bridge, who will control border-smuggling-all this will be decided in the dark of the night. In this competition for making as much money as possible, there will be a strange but peaceful co-existence, there will be no clash, just division of the booty. Sometimes there will be a press statement-just to assert one's political status. After all this is what politics is all about! We have became the enemy of the society, the class enemy, the reactionary, because we raise our voice against this system. I believe that some people find it distasteful to even utter our name.

We are not at all ashamed because of this. Our question is-what will the new generation get from the politicians who are dragging society towards destruction and ruin. Instead of job opportunities will they be given the right to become carriers of contraband? will they be given education or the right to become criminals? Who holds the reins of future politics? Is it a crime to be poor? Persons who turn a section of the unemployed people into criminals and use them, instead of guiding them to a better life, should realize one thing-one day the gun barrel of these criminals will be turned on them. People's united protest is more powerful than any firearm. Plenty of effort has been made to silence the organised protest of the people; more such effort will be made in future, but there must not be any fear. One must not stop dreaming of overcoming all obstacles and move ahead. The assembled mass at Saheed Minar on the first anniversary of 21st July proved this. I hope they will do so in future also.

The future will only show what it has in store for us. For the present, I have realized that somebody has to take the risk if one wants to bell the cat. Criticism, assault and injury have to be tolerated, sacrifices have to be made. No experience is unworthy of being remembered. My conscience does not sleep, but this book is an attempt to bring new awareness to my conscience. I have referred to some of the experiences. I express my reverence for those who have worked for the people's welfare and made sacrifices irrespective of their political affiliations. I condemn and condemn those professional politicians for whom politics serves as the means to amassing wealth and luxuries.

2

SOME EXPERIENCES AS A MEMBER OF PARLIAMENT

With the People's blessings I got the passport to the Parliament. Many have an idea of the new arena that I entered and the experiences I had. Again there are many who are eager to know about the role of Members and their conduct. Mainly for these people, the latent desire to write this book has been in my mind for a long time. Unless the experiences gathered before and after joining the Parliament are brought to light, unknown facts and truths will continue to remain outside the reach of many. If aspiring Parliamentarians get to know some facts and truths, this experience will give them the clues to many unknown realms. When I did not have any plans in my life of becoming a member of Parliament (in fact I did not have the chance to think of even being a member of the Vidhan Sabha), then I used to think "Oh my goodness, it is such a tremendous affair!"

It was through college elections that I got introduced to political electioneering. On both occasions, nobody stood against me and I was elected unopposed. My fellow students were very fond of me. This proves to be a great advantage in college elections. Students elect that person who mixes with others and has good relationship with everyone.

This matter is however related to the small boundaries of college. The municipal, Vidhan Sabha and Lok Sabha elections are different. The area covered for each such election escalates gradually from the small to the vast. I remember quite clearly that after 1982 I used to go to the Vidhan Sabha quite often. I would watch very carefully, from the Visitors' Gallery, how the MLA's delivered their speeches and raised issues regarding various problems. Regarding Parliament, however, I had neither the experience nor any idea. I had always heard that Parliament is a huge affair and covers such a vast area that it is like a huge labyrinth. At the first attempt it is very difficult to know one's way out.

Before becoming a member, I had not had the opportunity to see the Parliament. However, I had gone to Delhi many times, but most of the visits were in connection with political programmes. When the people of Jadavpur elected me with political programmes. When the people of Jadavpur elected me with their affectionate blessings, I felt scared, knowing that I would have to go to the Parliament. When the countless people of Jadavpur, and my colleagues were besides themselves with joy, I had withdrawn into a shell. It was as if I was facing a "dreadful prospect".

I was like a lost traveller being sent to an unknown wayside inn. How would I reach the place? I was subject to some undefined apprehension.

In 1984, sixteen persons of the Congress party were elected to the Lok Sabha from West Bengal. Together, we travelled in the same plane. Pranabda was the Finance Minister at that time, and he was in charge of us. He had sent Sree M. K. Mukherjee, the trusted person from his office, to look after us. Since we did not have any place to stay in at Delhi, arrangements for shared accomodation were made for myself and Late Indumati Bhattacharjee. The election of the leader was to be held the next day.

Pranabda escorted us to the Central Hall. So, there was no problem. On the first day I looked around a bit. During the next few days Ratanda (Ratan Mukherjee) and his wife, Moloya, helped me a great deal. My direct participation in the People's Court had begun.

Initially, things were beyond my comprehension. I would think Oh God, where have I come to? I was a novice and there was nobody to help and show the way.

I used to think that this (Parliament) was the ideal shrine where the voice is raised only in the interest of the People. I would think that each and everyone was very important. How fluently they would speak in English and quote from the Constitution! They were like Lord Narayan-holding the House captive in their role of the saviour of the people. With regret I used to think- If only I could be like them." I used to feel helpless and neglected. Having been trusted with the responsibility, would I be able to safeguard the honour of this same responsibility?

On the one hand I went about getting to know the Parliament, the Member and the Rules. On the other hand I was preparing myself so that the wisdom of experience would take me away from the slippery path of darkness and carry me to the coveted goal.

For 7 days I watched. At this juncture, I have to add

something. In the case of all political parties (other than the Congress party), newly elected Members of Parliament are helped a lot by their senior colleagues. They teach the new member the rules and protocol and instil self confidence in the new member. They should be thanked, but in our party (Congress party) the speciality is that each one should fend for himself.

I remember that I had to board a plane for the first time in my life not to travel within the country, but to go abroad. In 1983, I went to Kuala Lampur as an INTUC delegate to the seminar of the International Confederation of Trade Union (in short ICFTU). Subrata Mukherjee had recommended my name. Before this, a training camp for the INTUC Women's Wing had been organised at Delhi, Nearly 50 ladies from different parts of the country attended the 7 days camp. On the last day the All-India President of INTUC Sree Ramanujam attended the camp. He was an highly educated and experienced labour leader and had authored several useful books on labour problems. A question-answer session was handled by him. I answered all his questions correctly. As a result he had sent me to the ICFTU seminar.

That was my first plane journey. I had made up my mind to quietly pick up from my fellow passengers whatever was required to be done during the flight without letting anybody know. The flight by Thai Airways to Bangkok was followed by a 2 hours wait for the plane to Kuala Lampur. As it is I knew nothing and on top of it, it was a foreign country. I descended from the aircraft with trepidation. Then I saw a girl waiting with the "Kuala Lampur" placard. As soon as I spoke to her, she escorted me and a few others to a separate sitting-place. After two hours she put us on the Kuala Lampur bound flight.

On reaching Kuala Lampur I was in another fix. It

seems my life is tied to struggle, problems and obstacles all the way. Nobody from the organiser's side had come to receive me. It was nearly midnight; I was wondering what to do. I could not ask anybody a thing. The one factor that I could bank upon was the programme chart that showed our place of stay as South East Asian Hotel. I encashed a travellers' cheque at the airport and proceeded towards the hotel in a taxi on my own. While crossing the subway alone, at that late hour, it occurred to me that I had taken a great risk and could get killed. In which case, I would be indentified as an Indian from my passport, and if that was not found then nobody would get to know of my fate.

I ultimately reached the hotel. While I was enquiring at the Reception Desk the organisers came running and begged forgiveness. Since they had made a mistake about the time schedule, I had no regrets. After all, why fear when the hurdle had been crossed.

Perhaps referring to the incident is out of context; but it is experiences which pave the way of life after all. In a somewhat parallel manner I made it to the Parliament after the death of Indiraji. I silently observed everything for 7 days inside the House, then I decided, right or wrong, I would have to project myself as a people's representative through my own efforts.

I raised my hand during the **QUESTION HOUR**; I was not permitted to ask a question. I became very angry when I was overlooked the following day also. The next morning I entered the Parliament, determined to voice my protest strongly, come what may, in case I was not allowed to speak. Inevitably, I was ignored. I rose and said, "Hon'ble Speaker Sir, everyday I am raising my hand, why don't you allow me to ask a question." The Speaker, rather bewildered at my action, then gave me the permission to speak. It was about the distribution of unconditional land deeds to refugees. This was an election pledge, hence my question. The Speaker said, "You are a new comer, perhaps that is why you don't know the Rules. The question under discussion pertains to enemy property, and your question has no connection with it." I retorted, "If there is no connection, why are you not allowing the half-an-hour discussion as per Parliamentary Procedures?" On that day probably I had not been able to keep my emotions in check, and my question must have revealed my sincerity. The Speaker, almost in the manner of an affectionate father, gave his permission. I felt as though I had conquered the Heavens.

Even though the request for half-an-hour discussion had been made by me, I had not known that I would not necessarily get the chance to speak. In the Lok Sabha, starting from questionnaires, everything is decided by ballot i.e. a type of lottery system where the person first picked from the pooled names starts the discussion. I started praying to God, "After giving me this opportunity please do not forsake me." May be it was ordained by destiny that my prayers would be heard because the very first name that was picked up was mine. The rest is history, as the people of Bengal know. Voluminuous data, enquiries, deliberations and effort, arguments and counterarguments not with standing, the people's demand triumphed. Of course, the refugees would not have received the unconditional land deeds without the support and unstinted cooperation of our late leader Rajivji.

Many may think that I hail from erstwhile East Bengal (now Bangladesh), and it is because of this that I have a special attachment towards the refugees from East Bengal. This is not so. My family members and I have never differentiated between people of the two "Bengals" (i.e. East & West Bengal). Both are equally dear to us and are our soulmates. West Bengal is my birthplace and my work place. I have never had an opportunity to go to Bangladesh. Just as our National Anthem, written by Rabindra Nath Tagore, cannot be separated from our heart, so also his song "Amar Sonar Bangla, Ami tomai Valobashi" brings to our mind the image of Sk Mujibur Rehman and the liberation struggle (of Bangladesh). It is as though he is still alive amidst the struggle for liberation in any corner of the World. That is why petty geographical differences should be set aside and our foremost identity ought to be that we are just human beings.

Perhaps I am writing excessively about my thoughts. In truth, my pent up thoughts wish to pour out at the touch of the pen. This cannot be denied.

There are some members whose appearance may lack smartness, who do not speak English with the anglicised accent; but these members are very active and make honest attempts to speak for the welfare of the people. However these members rarely get the opportunity. It occurs to me repeatedly that Members are divided into two distinct classes. There is a special group of members who, while addressing the Chair, keep their main focus on the press gallery, for the sake of publicity. The other "ordinary" class lacks "glamour"; hence they are less important. It seems that they are there to mark their presence only. This makes me feel very sad and reminds me of the concept of "first class citizen" and "second class citizen". In spite of their good intentions the ordinary members do not receive the "importance" and the people of their constituencies think of them as ineffective Parliamentarians. It is precisely for this reason that most members stay away from the House except during the Zero and Question Hours. Even though the actual people's representation is in the Lok Sabha, the scope for discussions is more in the

Rajya Sabha because the latter has fewer members. Sometimes a member is unable to raise important issues in the Lok Sabha due to inadequate time.

The Lok Sabha Members can make two typed of question-verbal and written. Unlike written questions, where the reply comes in answer form only, in the case of verbal questions, one gets the opportunity to directly enquire from the concerned minister. There is a section in the Lok Sabha which selects the questions for discussions from both types that are submitted by the members. It also decided which ones will be 'verbal' and which ones will be "starred'. It is seen on numerous occasions that questions related to people's welfare and "collective" problems are not selected as starred questions, many queries on personal matters, evidently unrelated to people's problems come up. I don't want to blame anybody for this.

If I speak against the age old system, then the "Privilege" action will be initiated against me, but for the benefit of the people, I am prepared to face it. After all, the Mahabharat will not lose it's sanctity if personal views are expressed about Parliament. Personally I feel that people do have the right to discuss the shortcomings and faults of 'Janatar Durbar'. After all it is exists for the welfare of the people and runs on funds of the people.

Though the idiom "where there is a will, there is a way" does not always work, one does hope for some results. To strengthen one's will and conviction Swami Vivekananda had advised"To succeed, you must have tremendous perseverence and will power. "I will drink the ocean" says the persevering soul" and at my will the mountains will crumble". Have that sort of energy, that sort of will, work hard, and you will reach the goal".

Some persons become Members of this Durbar not on the Strength of selflessness, forbearance, honesty and sincerity, but on the basis of glamour, money and muscle power and, in some cases, organisational strength. After their electoral victory, some members have only one goal-like selfish giants they forget about people's welfare and serve their benefactors who had contributed to their campaign fund.

In the past renowned personalities have added lustre to the Janata's Durbar with their novel ideas, achievements, sincerity and ever-shining value based principles. There are still such personalities, but their number has gone down. The public sense of awareness is increasing, people judge candidates not by their party ideologies but on the basis of their credibility.

Now the Janatar Durbar has become a sophisticated weapon through which power can be misused. There are many who do this and there are many such instances.

These political gangleaders have total disregard for the law. They are like the temporary leaseholder, who extracts every ounce of what power can give. They have brought disgrace to the Parliament in countless ways. It is due to such persons that even the honest and good members get a bad name. There is an increasing trend of the blatant use of influential person's names to get one's job done.

People should get to know of this; I am briefly narrating a couple of incidents. The Central Government had taken a decision to close down the Govt. of India Press in Bengal, Himachal Pradesh and other part of the country. At that time I was MP from Jadavpur. The employees of the Presss had approached me for help. After thorough investigation, I found out that for the sole benefit of a certain ringleader an extreme injustice was going to be committed. In the Parliamnet, I requested for a Half-an-Hour discussion and this was allowed.

The Half-an-Hour Discussion is normally held at 5 p.m.. Armed with papers and documents, I went to the Parliament. The then Parliamentary Affairs Minister, Smt. Sheila Dixit had been ringing me up all the morning, requesting me not to be present at the Lok Sabha. The reason being that my participation in the discussions would embarass the Government. I had immediately understood. If I exposed the details, the cat would come out of the bag. That is why there was no lack of pleading and humbleness from the Minister's side. I have a certain stubborn streak; once I take a decision I never backtrack. I went to the house.

Seeing no other way out, the concerned Minister approached the Parliamentary Affairs Minister. He was banking on the fact that whatever Smt. Dixit said as Parliamentary Affairs minister would be a Party whip and according to Party norms, one would have to obey the order. Anyhow, Minister called me and requested me not to bring up the issue. I was adamant-I would have to speak out in the interest of the people. Besides this, I would be betraying the people if I did not speak out inspite of the matter being listed in Parliament Business.

Finding no alternative, Minister tried to intimidate me by saying that the Prime Minister, Rajivji, had sent word that I should not raise the issue. Again, using names to get things done. It was not difficult to see through the conspiracy.

The PM was in his Parliamentary Office. I met his Personal Secretary, Mr. George. The Parliamentary Affairs Minister was unaware of this. I directly asked Georgeji whether there were any strictures or instructions from Rajivji. George told me "I will find out and let you know within 10 minutes". Exactly within 10 minutes I was informed by George that Rajivji had given no such instructions! Can you imagine it. A Parliamentary Affairs Minister was using the PM's name to back up a lie.

The House resumed as usual and I was present. Both the Ministers had thought that I would not be as per their wishes. When they saw me, it seemed as though they were seeing an apparition. I was thinking of how both had been put in their right places.

The discussions started. Everything was turning topsy turvy for the Minister. It was as though a storm had swept through the Parliament and the Minister's neatly coiffured hair was truly wind blown.

There was a delay in coming to a decision, and at one point I declared that if the decision was to close the Govt. of India Press, then I would "walkout". The Minister received another jolt. A tug of war ensued; ultimately the Minister was compelled to announce that the Press would not be closed immediately and the issue would be reviewed.

There are countless such instances of the Member ultimately not turning up to raise listed questions. The matter is different when a Member absents due to personal exigencies, but in many cases the give and take adjustments are an undeniable fact.

In a democratic set up the opposition parties are given a lot of importance. Compared to the opportunities they get for raising issues, discussion and placing proposals, the treasury bench members hardly get a fraction. I know of many instances where a certain section uses such opportunities with finesse. They become partners in this game of give and take and reap the golden harvest.

An idealist in this scenario! How astonishing! Surely this is impossible. Any immense concern for the people is like a smokescreen behind which there is no urgency or inclination towards doing anything good. What really exists is a chronicle of betrayal of the people which hides under cover of a half-baked idealist.

Is it wrong to criticise the members whose sole interest is self gratification inspite of their commitment towards the people? Is it that such characters are a "privileged class" and all their faults are to be overlooked? What is the harm in restoring values in politics by exposing the truth to the people?

Amitabh Bachchan was the focal point of a lot of hue and cry when he was a Member of the Parliament. He was forced to leave politics. I have heard him twice in the Parliaent. He used to be very serious and his actor's image would never show. I have heard Sunil Dutt speak on national integration. He shows restraint and intellect. Both of them had left behind their "actor's image". Madhu Dadavate, Indrajit Gupta, Geeta Mukherjee have impressed me with their impeccable conduct and oration.

When I was representing Jadavpur constituency, there were noisy scenes within the Parliament everyday. Madhu Dandavate had once asked me what was my diet and what was the source of my strength. I had retorted that my diet was the same as his but my strength was my electorate. This had made him laugh.

Parliament has tradition. Whatever the arguments and differences of opinion inside the House, once outside, in the Central Hall such things are set aside when members sit beside each other to chat. Then comaderie prevails and many amusing incidents happen.

Bholanath Sen was a MP then and as a barrister he had an additional income. There is a 'Bengali corner' in the Central Hall where all the members from Bengal would sit together. Whenever Bholada came to the Central Hall I would order snacks, in jest, for everyone. When the bill arrived a couple of us would chant "happy birthday to Bholada", thereby giving him the hint to pay the bill. This was all preplanned. We got to celebrate his birthday countless times in a month.

Though, at times, in the Parliament, there are terribly heated and intense exchanges and arguments, in the Central Hall it is entirely different. Here the atmosphere is relaxed. Since I maintain good relations not only with members from Bengal but members from other states also, I have to often join them for coffee. In Central Hall everybody is very friendly.

Amongst all the members, Santosh Mohan Dev enjoys chit chatting the most. He is fond of eating and treating others also. Lately, he has started a "corner" in the Central Hall for the members from the North-East India.

It is here that everybody keeps an eye on which way the wind is blowing in Indian politics. It is the hub of political discussions and news. Everyone keeps tabs on the others. That is why the Ministers try to avoid the Hall. A special watch is kept on who speaks to a member of the ruling party who is currently out of grace. When one is useful, he is no a saint and when he is no longer of use he becomes a rascal! Even the minimum level of courtesy is forgotten amidst the arrogance that power begets. A combination of political ups and downs and degeneration in civilised behaviour is evident here.

It is true that many members do bring to the Minister's notice in many matters. In 60% of such cases, the Government does assure that the issue will be considered or gives a decision. And, it is only when the people's interest are looked after in this way that Parliament shows its true splendour and glory.

Parliament will exist inspite of all the arguments, disagreements, agreements, and the rise or fall of the Parties. One Party will come to power, another will go out, but as long as the spirit of democracy lives unimpaired, Parliament will want to stay alive and vibrant for then only is the people's interest being served.

With humbleness this book brings forth some questions. In what manner can the much cherished honour of Parliament be protected? Will humanitarianism's eternal light shine in this decadent, gloomy path?

Only people who believe in value based politics deserves a place in the Parliament. Political parties have a crucial role to play in this aspect. The voter's awareness is also a must. What is required is electoral reforms to be made by the Election Commission so that deserving candidates are elected. Let the candidate's worth be evaluated by their willingness to work, ability to learn and experience. Such qualities will be able to guide the people towards the future.

Nowadays the general idea is that representation from the so-called sophisticated class is necessary. At the threshold of the 21st century this culture may be necessary, but this is not the only qualification that is reqired. What is also required is knowing one's country and its people and to sincerely realise their problems. Our former Prime Minister, respected Lal Bahadur Shastri came from a peasant's family. He was shortstatured but had tremendous sense of values. It was he who raised the slogan "Jai Jawan, Jai Kishan" (Hail the soldier, Hail the farmer). For this he did not have to cultivate any pseudo mannerisms. He had realised that the country's all round development would not be possible if the rural regions continued to be overlooked, because 70% of the population lives in the rural areas. Knowing about the urban problems is necessary, but knowing the real picture of India's agrarian economy is of foremost importance.

I have expressed some of my feelings. This might hurt the interests of many, but it is not aimed against any particular person. If necessary, for the sake of the people more facts will be revealed.

There is still a long way to go, hence the pace, at present, is slow, steady and restrained. For the sake of values this pace will pick up in the future. There will be many opportunities to perceive the future through present experiences.

I am also a member of this Parliament. Let the people judge me by my conduct and life-style. The common man has the right to judge. I do not have the audacity to say that I am 100% correct. The people's voice is the true call, and even if it holds me back, I will consider it as their blessing.

If these submissions of mine leave the slightest mark in your minds, then what I have felt and perceived will be worth it. I quote Rabindra Nath Tagore:

> "My birth is worthwhile
>
> Because I have been born in this land
>
> Oh my Mother! My birth is worthwhile because I have loved you."

There are some senior members of the Parliament whom I personally respect. On many occasions, everybody agrees with their way of thinking, ideological differences nothwithstanding. Certain members express their political views and raise objections, just for the sake of doing so.

In the Parliament, if one pays adequate attention, many undercurrents can be perceived.

I distinctly remember something about Vijayantimala when she was a member of the Lok Sabha. Her husband would be present in the Visitors' gallery as long as she would be in the House. Everytime she spoke, she would look at her husband and Dr. Bali would nod his approval. Family members of some members and Ministers also turn up for the same purpose.

The gallery is packed up specially when the Finance Budget and Railway Budget are presented in the Parliament. The House becomes full of life on these occasions. In case a no-confidence motion is taken up, the gallery becomes overcrowded.

Sometimes school children come to watch from the Visitor's Gallery. If they see the leaders arguing and quarreling, they return disappointed. During the last session virtually no work was done. When I joined after a 6 months gap, the House functioned for only three days. One day about fifty school girls came to see the House. As soon as the Speaker entered, there was bedlam. Seeing the situation. the Speaker adjourned the House and left. Some Members of the Treasury and Opposition benches started to blame each other and almost came to blows. I was watching the children's expressions. They had come with high hopes of watching the Question Hour session. Instead, they were witnessing the Members coming to blows! The school girls started running, and in their haste to get away, they toppled over each other. The Members did not think even once about the impact of this experience on the children. The scene was certainly not enjoyable.

There is one thing over which the Members show a lot of patience. Whenever our counterparts from other countries visit the Parliament, all Members, irrespective of their party affiliations, stick to a certain 'tradition'. This is a good sign in parliamentary democracy.

It is in this House that I have seen people jumping

down from the gallery on top of Members to press home their 'demands'. The alert security guards immediately detain them for questioning. They are released only if the security personnel are satisfied and that, after the day's business is over.

Such incidents cause a minor storm; the speaker does not pay attention to this and after a couple of minutes the situation goes back to normal.Just imagine a situation where a person jumps upon a Member who has cardiac problems. Such incidents can cause fatal heart attacks.

These intrusions are a part of a 'tradition'. It has occurred before and will occur in future. People who can carry this out, inspite of the tight security, do so to draw the attention of the House to their demands.

Just as the mingling of all caste, creed and religion brightens the proceedings of the House, incidents of such trespassing also brighten up the House.

Parliament is the repository of such astonishing and strange incidents.

3

FIGHT FOR HUMAN RIGHTS

Human Rights-the most precious facet of human values and principles is inseparable from fundamental rights. In order to define human rights one has to first ask "who is a man?" The answer is "a member of the human family"! When the combination of honour and reasoning develops within man the latent elements of conscience and senses grow within him. This becomes more significant than physical prowess and man's real qualities and abilities are harnessed towards worthwhile activities. It is through human rights that human values spreads its branches and grows into a colossal tree.

Primitive men lived in the forests. They ate fruits and meat (raw or roasted). Their lives depended on the bounty of nature. The light of civilisation could not penetrate them. Their predominant characteristic was tremendous physical prowess. Then, one day, time's unfailing progression reached the much desired light of civilisation to them;

the dominating characteristic of physical strength paled into insignificance and Man's mental faculties blossomed forth as civiliasation's victorious march brought enlightment to him. Having become a part of the transformation process of civilisation, the primitive man revealed himself in a new way. The origin of the Indian lifestream is to be found in this path of progress of civilasation.

It was amidst the mango orchards of Plassey that India lost her freedom in 1757. The English traders became the rulers. For 190 years the Indians, chained and bound to subjugation, had only one desire to free their motherland from the prisons of British domination. After a long struggle, came the much awaited independence. The prison doors broke down, the darkness of subjugation gave way to light as the sun of Indian's independence rose. This was followed by the birth of the Indian Constitution-the guardian of citizens' rights. The Constitution was written under the stewardship of Dr B. R. Ambedkar (Chairman of the committee entrusted with this task). Other leaders joined to complete the work. Based on the principles of moral values, the constitution ensures for the citizens social, economic and political equality; it gives freedom to follow one's religion, profession, education and culture; it guarantees freedom of speech and expression. The duties and responsibilities of the citizens are clearly laid down. While dealing with the citizens' rights and duties, the Preamble to the constitution has clearly stated; "We THE PEOPLE OF INDIA, having solemnly resolved to constitute India into a SOVEREIGN SOCIALIST SECULAR DEMOCRATIC REPUBLIC and to secure to all its citizens:

JUSTICE, social, economic and political

LIBERTY of thought, expression, belief, faith and worship

EQUALITY Of status and of opportunity; and to promote among them all

FRATERNITY assuring the dignity of the individual and the unity of the nation". The Constitution operates as a fundamental law. When people are denied their constitutional rights, the peple's revolution against injustice rages like the tempest. Just as the "where, when and how" of this tempest cannot be explained, it is also not possible to say to what extent it will spread. When torture, lawlessness, injustice, persecution and contempt throw human rights to the dust, when human rights is heartlessly trampled upon, the latent conscience rises and strikes the human heart like waves of the ocean. At this point protest expresses itself in many words and ways. When the rights, instead of being the sentinel, assumes the role "seek and extort", then the strom is bound to rise against violation of human rights. This storm will weed out and throw away the parasites and extortionists and cry out aloud **"REVOLT, REVOLT FROM ALL CORNERS"**. The fiery heart will say

"Battle-weary Revolutionary

I will be at peace on that day

When the plaintive cry of the oppressed will no longer be heard in the wind and sky."

Just as ashes cannot diffuse a fire, and the hand cannot hold back the rays of sunlight, so also the human mind's most precious facet, the pure human philosophy, can never be extinguished. It may be trampled upon for a short period of time, but one day it breaks the shackles of the demonic cruelty and sings the victory song of humanitarianism. It is Parliament which provides the base from where the highest levels of humanitarianism can be reached.

The alter of parliamentary democracy will be marked

with shame unless, (in larger interest and for sake of ideals) ideological differences are surmounted and certain ideals and moral values are adopted in the struggle for existence. Narrowness in outlook and mind must also be left behind. In a democracy, the constitutional rights and fundamental rights are bound inseparably. However, it will not be fit and proper to enjoy the benefits of these rights alone; there are directives about the duties to which citizens must abide. In the interest of our country, people and society, we must remember a saying of Mahatma Gandhi

"Let communalism be our main enemy. Let secularism be our main foundation. Let Nationalism be our main politics. Let humanism be our main religion. Let patriotism be our main ideal."

Human rights has a connection with moral rights, if human rights is to be established and protected, then moral values must be given importance. The genesis of human rights lies in giving due respect to moral values. That is why human and moral rights are interlinked.

The English Bill of Rights followed by the American Declaration of Independence and the French Revolution's proclamation of Rights of Man were all based on the general concept of mankind's overall rights. In India, Parliament passed the Protection of Human Rights Act on 8.1.94. "Human Rights' have been defined in section 2(d) of the Act and mean the rights relating to life, liberty, equality and dignity of the individual guaranteed by the constitution or embodies in the international covenants and enforceable by courts in India.

Apart from this "The Universal declaration of Human Rights" was adopted in December 1984, with India's participation. India is also a signatory to the international covenant on economic, social and cultural right of 1966. Article 51 of the constitution as one of the Directive Principles of the state policies states that the state shall endeavour to foster respect for international peace and treaty obligations. In addition to this Article 20(3) of the constitution which is one of the fundamental rights of our citizens and the 125 years old Indian Evidence Act (1872) has provided that confession before a police officer would not be taken as evidence.

At this juncture a question arises in the minds of many- what suddenly prompted me to go on a 'Dharna' with my colleagues for 21 days on the public throughfare of Calcutta? Of couse, there was contempt, ridicule and misbehaviour from a handful. The language in which comments were made by certain leftist leaders were in bad taste. It seemed as though raising the issue of violation of human rights was by itself a violation of human rights. Not doing wrong was itself wrongful.

Killing inside lock-up or death in police custody is the highest in Bengal. Yet, the state Government is not at all bothered.

"Helpless people are drowning

They do not know how to swim".

It is true that all persons in the administration are not of the same mould. The question that invariably arises isWhy should people be subject to inhuman mental and physical torture by a section of the administration just to serve the latters' interest? One must remember that the guardians of law (police) are not above the law.

The police force maintains law and order with the help of two Acts mainly. One is the Indian Penal Code (or IPC) and the other is the Criminal Procedure Code. According to the Criminal Procedure Code Sec 161, the police can interrogate a detainee but cannot torture him.

Although they do not have the right to torture, in most cases they do beat up the detainess. That is why the law provides for the punishment of the guilty policemen (IPC Sec 330, 331 and CPC Sec 197). Causing physical injuries for the purpose of extracting proof of guilt is a punishable offence for policemen. In such cases, the punishment can go upto seven years.

The Police Regulation of Bengal 1943 (PRB) Sec 262 mentions that steps have to be taken against torture in police custody. This regulation clearly makes the officers in charge of Police Stations responsible for the safety of those detained under police custody. Torture of detainess under police custody is prohibited under the Calcutta Police Rules 1866 Sec 10(3) and District Police Rules 1866 (Sec 8). The directives make it obligatory for the police to provide shelter and food to detainees. The constitution (Article 21) clearly states that the police do not have the right to cause the death of detainees. The right to Personal freedom and right to life are also categorically stated in this Article. The Indian Government has, from time to time, issued directives for prevention of police torture and use of third degree methods on detainees. On the one hand the police will expect the people to abide by laws of the land and on the other hand they themselves will violate laws-this cannot be tolerated.

Instead, a human attitude, love and affection on the part of the administration can encourage many anti-socials to reform and make a new life. About 60% of anti-socials can turn over a new leaf if their conscience can be aroused. Alongside, Rabindranath Tagore's words must also be remembered:

With the indicted

If the judge also weeps and feels equal pain,
That is justice at its very best"

The National Human Rights Commission has reported that the number of deaths in police custody is the highest in West Bengal. The true character of the persons who had ridiculed us and spoken ill of us came to my mind repeatedly during the dharna. West Bengal's the then Minister in charge of the Police (who is also the Chief Minister) should remember 28.10.1987. On that date, while inaugurating the Tangra Police Station, this same person (Jyoti Basu) had said that death under police custody does not occur in any civilised nation. On 7.7.1971 Jyoti Basu and Hare Krishna Konar had written to the then Central Minister, S.S. Ray "Dont you know that there are charges of murder against the O.C. Jorabagan and the DC North and they continue to be on duty and remain the pet officers of the ruling party".

At the time of the election to Vidhan Sabha (1977), the CP(I)M's 36 point manifesto had promised investigation of all deaths in police and jail custody and in 'confrontations' of 1970-77. They had promised punishment of the guilty. Keeping this in view, the Hartosh Chakraborty and Sharma Commission was formed. What happened to the investigation of these committees? Has a single police officer been punished?

The year 1991 The congress party was in power in Andhra Pradesh. While reporting about an incident of torture to the Governor, P. Soundaraiya, Hanumant Rao, Gadhadar Rao, B.A. Reddy [of the CP(I)M-CITU Agricultural Labour Union) commented to their memorandum "Beating under police custody is a crime and violation of human rights"...The turn of events showed that destiny had her last laugh. Those champions for the cause of human rights now described our dharna in Bengal as a "drama" and "gimmick". These same persons became the sentinels of the torture chambers. This is at a time when all other nations are discussing and introducing legal safeguards for ensuring human rights.

The Bill of Rights has the following to say while defining nature of fundamental rights:

"A fundamental right is so called because it is secured not by the ordinary law, but a fundamental law which in modern times is embodied in a written constitution that cannot be altered by the ordinary process of legislation".

Therefore, fundamental rights is a moral right and the steps that lead to this is human rights. If the guardians of law can play the role of the extortionist inspite of so many laws, then doubts arise about the very existence of human values.

Inspite of the directives of the Supreme Court and high court should the tug of war between man and annihilators continue? Why should helpless and poor persons have to face inhuman torture just because they are not able to offer bribes to a section of the police? Even before he is pronounced guilty, by the court, why should man be exposed to such animal-like frenzied torture where his eyes are gouged, or nails are ripped out with iron tongs or burning cigarette butts are used to cause burns all over his body? Will the guardians of law, be allowed to assume the role of the executioner and unleash such nightmare after having sold their souls to a certain Party? Will the oppressed people's cry of agony only break its head on the stone walls of the prisons in vain?

In most cases (lock-up deaths) the following information is sent to the victim's family:

The detainee has committed suicide

or

he died while trying to escape from the police

or

he succumbed to some serious illness.

The old mother, widow and minor children don't even realise how "injustie in the name of justice" has ruined them. Not knowing what to do, they gaze helplessly and their tears wash away their will-power. Will such incidents happen one after the other and the people of Bengal not raise the slogan for emancipation?

I have received reports of many such incidents. Whenever I received these reports I have the matter investigated by persons I trust. If I find the report to be genuine, I take up the matter, but I do not do this to victimize anyone nor to get political mileage. The moral aspect of human values inspired and guides my actions.

Sk. Azad (of Garden Reach, Calcutta) died in police lock-up on 1st January, 1995. I have heard the details of the horrible torture that Azad had been subjected to, from his mother and young widow. When they came to my residence on 2nd January, 1995, I had gone out. It was only when I had rung up my office (at my residence) over an urgent matter, I was informed by Manik that Sk. Azad's pregnant widow had come over to my residence with some relatives. They wanted me to go over to Garden Reach once to see marks of torture on Azad's body. They had decided not to bury him until I went ever. I immediately instructed that they should return home. I also informed them that I would go to their residence in the evening.

Accordingly, I proceeded to Azad's residence in the evening. With me were Biman Banerjee (advocate) Rantideb Sengupta, News Reporter of Bartaman, and my colleague

Sonali Guha. The news-media on the whole, did not know that I was going to Garden Reach. When I am in Calcutta, the press reporters come to me everyday and as a routine matter, that day, just as I was starting for Azad's house, Rantideb Sengupta and Rohit Basu (of Ananda Bazar Patrika) had reached my place. So, four of us travelled in one car, Rohit and a photographer (of Ananda Bazar Patrika) followed us in another car. At that time none of us knew that I would again come face to face with death.

The CP(I)M party had no scheduled meeting along the route we took, but they were holding a small meeting on the pavement. As soon as they saw me in the car they rushed on to the road. The armed CP(I)M cadres encircle our car in the presence of the police. It took them a few seconds to smash the glass windows and windscreen with stones and bricks. They had kept ready some dust mixed with poison in a packet. This mixture was thrown on our faces and eyes. After this, they tried to pull me out of the car and a tussle followed. Everything seemed dark, we could not see anything. The shattered glass had caused injuries to Rantideb, Biman Banerjee, Sonali and Rantideb was bleeding profusely. In the melee, the door got jammed. Having failed to pull me out through the door, they rained blows on me through the broken window. A brick, thrown through the shattered windscreen hit me on the chest.

Biman Banerjee tried in vain to start the car. The police stood as mute spectators as 50 CP(I)M hooligans, bent on an orgy of human sacrifice encircled the car.

My body was covered with shredded glass and splinters entered my eyes. Even in that state I kept on telling Biman Banerjee not to start the car and drive away. I wanted to 'see' to what extent they intended to injure me! Then came the climax-they aimed at me and fired. By God's unseen hand the bullet pierced through the hand of a passerby a muslim youth named Akhtar. By now Biman Banerjee was desperately trying to start the car. Suddenly it started and we were on our way amidst a hail of gunshots.

We headed for the hospital. How was the blueprint prepared to remove me from the scene? The CP(I)M had come to know through the Administration about my intention to visit Garden Reach. They had made preparations. The main point to note is that we were not allowed to go near Azad's house. We were not allowed to see the marks on Azad's body. Why? To shield whom? The man who was identified as the No. 1 culprit in our FIR was not arrested. Instead the police guarded his house! It was a shameful episode as far as democratic rights are concerned. It had certainly cast a black mark on Bengal's democracy and moral values.

Some incidents that took place in Rajerhat Police Station have left a deep impression in my mind. There is a certain person who stays there and this police station is completely under his command. There is also a certain police officer who 'picks up' people according to his whim and fancy. Then he threatens that if they work for the Congress Party, they will be locked up in 'dungeons' of the P.S.

After three consecutive lock-up deaths in this police station Sukhen Chakravarty, Tanmoy and Prabir approached me and according to their request I addressed a public meeting in that locality. In that meeting I told the guardians of law not to misuse the law. However, "theives do not pay heed to religious stories," and incidents continued unabetted. I was also keeping watch. The police (wilful as they are) never realised that we would be able to collect all the information.

The day before the general strike, Munwar Ali was

murdered in a preplanned manner. As usual, the family was informed that Munwar had committed suicide by hanging himself in the police lock-up room. The news came to me from Rajerhat. When I enquired whether there were any marks of injury on his body, I was immediately informed that there were many burn marks. That happened to be the day of the general strike (called by the Congress party). So I instructed from my residence that coloured photographs of different parts of the dead body were to be taken and sent over to me. I also instructed Jyotipriyo Mallick and Alok Das (Secretaries of the State Committee of Youth Congress) to take the dead body to the police station and to gherao the police station. They were to be accompanied by Sukhen Chakravarty, Tanmoy, Prabir and others, and a complaint was to be lodged at the police station.

I scrutinised the photographs that had been sent to me. My suspicions over certain aspects grew:

1) The police had said that it was a case of suicide by hanging, but there were no marks on the neck. Even light bruise marks were not there.

2) The marks that were there clearly indicated that his toe and finger nails had been torn out.ci

3) It was clear that the toes, fingers and soles of the feet had been burnt.ci

4) There were black marks all over the body.

For the sake of argument someone can raise the question that the burns were inflicted afterwards. Firstly, under Islamic religious rites the dead body is not burnt, therefore, the reasoning is meaningless. Secondly, if the burning occures when the blood is still circulating in the body, the colour of the marks are quite different from the marks when burning occurs after death.

Therefore, Munwar Ali was a victim of torture in police custody. The police had stated that stolen goods worth one lakh rupees had been found in his shop.

When I reached late Munwar Ali's residence, the place was crowded with neighbours. I found that the 'residence' was a small room and the family used to survive with help from the neighbours. This fact had been suppressed and a story about the stolen goods and been concocted. The truth was something else. Munwar Ali had not been able to hand over the sum of money that he had been asked to give, consequently, he had died in police custody.

Such incidents have occurred in large numbers in all the districts of Bengal. In the past, the common people were not aware of these incidents. Prompt reporting by the newsmedia and collective action of different forums nowadays keep the public well informed. Some Human Rights organisations (especially ADPR) are also doing a lot in this sphere. Now that the Human Rights Commission has been established, there is greater awareness, and this also makes it impossible to suppress many facts.

I hear of numerous incidents (often shrouded under a cloud of mystry) in connection with politics. The police know everything (the truth) but they cannot take action because of the political pressures from heavyweights of the ruling party. Sometimes sensational news hit the press headlines. Like, a notorious criminal is apprehended because of prompt action taken by a policeman. The secret behind this action remains unrevealed. Actually the criminal had flourished under the patronage of that policeman, and the arrest was a set-up job. The latter happens to be the infamous person who directly aided and abetted the murder of three young men at Bansdroni (South Calcutta). Now his target was Sree Gopal Roy, Councillor of Ward 113. If the truth is ever disclosed, the ringleader (who masterminded the three murders from behind the scenes) can be recognised, and whom inspite of being an employee of the police force, moves about with CPI(M)-backed anti-socials in his official motorcycle after mid-night. He has even handed over his police revolver to the CPI(M)-backed hoodlums. It may sound unbelievable, but it was in this way that the tripple murders were organised at Bansdroni. The common man cannot open his mouth because of fear psychosis, but this type of injustice cannot last long. Either today or tomorrow "MICHRI' will be exposed.

All these incidents stirred my mind and soul and I felt an yearning from within to do something. When the law enforcing machinery was assuming the role of the demon and ruining families, then it was imperative for the public to know about these families. Compensation from the State Government was also an urgent necessity that is, either a job for a member of the family or a minimum family pension of Rs. 1500/-. This is because the State Government can never evade it's moral responsibility over the deaths in police custody.

I, therefore, started the "Holy War" for protection of Human Rights. From the Prime Minister to the Chief Minister nobody had been able to say that this movement was irrelevant and that our demands were illogical. I know that the Chief Minister (of West Bengal) would not give anything worthwhile, but at the same time, I did not want the State Government to get the chance to say that they had not been contacted. Keeping this in view, Gyan Singh Sohanpal, Dr. Tarun Adhikary, Satya Bapuli and others had gone to the Chief Minister to submit out demands. Simultaneously, we had kept the Governor and the Prime Minister fully briefed. I also brought to the Prime Minister's notice that compensation ought to be paid to the families of the persons who died in police custody in other states of India.

I had not anticipated that the sit-in demonstration for Human Rights would continue round the clock for 21 days. It was done in the interest of humanity and was not confined within any political narrow-mindedness and arrogance.

I requested Sudip Bandopadhyay (MLA) to have the platform erected for the participants to sit on. Accordingly, the platform was set up in the heart of the city-Esplanade. The person who stood by us like a guardian was Sudip Bandopadhyay, MLA. Nehalbhai, Alauddin, Rajib, Asit and Bejoy all proved their dedication. Pankaj Banerjee, Sadhan Pandey, Sovanda, Bishuda, Amal Dutta, Roma Basu, Mala Roy, Parbati Devi, Smita Bakshi, Shukla Das, Kajal Banerjee, Aparna Neogi, Dibyendu Biswas, Durga Mukherjee, Nripen Banerjee, Anil Mukherjee and other leaders, Municipal Councillors, Members of local bodies, many organisations (some apolitical), poet Subhas Mukherjee, Phulrenu Guha, the senior Leftist leader Manoranjan Hazra and other leftists (who have not lost their conscience) all came and inspired and encouraged us.

My companions round the clock were Dilip Majumder, Councillor, Subrata Bakshi, Bani Singha Roy, Balu, Aloke, Mukul Roy, Sonali Guha, Ruma, Rita, Gopa, Krishna (Sr.), Sankari, Sandhya, Krishna, Protima (Sr.), Sudipa and many others. The other participants were Rathin Talukdar, Arup, Akbar, Tama, Tapan, Ujjal, Gopal, Sanjoy, Mana, Susanta, Mihir, Tilak, Robi, Akhil, Jabbar, Chaitanyamoy, Asima, Tapati, Bappan, Kala, Amar Bhattacharya and Ananta Bharati. Of course, Subrata Mukherjee, MLA, came to us often to encourage us. People would come in thousands everyday and the inclement weather conditions could not deter our spirits. The people had sanctified our "manch' with their blessings and it became the symbol of our beliefs and convictions. The Imam of Tipu Sultan Mosque and other Maulavis offered prayers for our Human Rights movement. Many affiliates of the SC-ST-OBC Organisations expressed their spontaneous solidarity. To the neglected sections of society, this platform took the form of a temple. The Dharna had started on 6th November, 1995. "Human Rights Day" was observed on 11th November, 1995 (Birth Anniversary of Maulana Abul Kalam Azad). Thousands of persons joined hands and stood side by side forming a human chain in the Esplanade-Park Street area. The fight against evil had found a new direction. On 15th November's 95, seven lakh people courted arrest peacefuly all over Bengal in a gesture of solidarity. While the Dharna was continuing, a two hours Blockade all over the State brought normal life to a standstill. For this inconvenience I offer my apologies to the people.

The action programmes went off peacefully one after another, but there was no reaction from the Administration. The discourteous conduct of the Leftist Government made one thing very clear-their 'revolution' and the demands that they had put forth at one time were merely an eyewash and a means for capturing power and winning elections.

We withstood the storms and torrential rains, and threw the threats that we received in the garbage heap. The 'Janata Darbar' (People's Court) continued to function from the same platform. On it separate enclosures were made, with the help of wooden partitions, for the 'Press Corner' and the 'People's Court'. Hundreds of letters were received at the Darbar everyday. The common man, having lost confidence in the mute and deaf Government, wrote about their problems. The Janatas Darbar was under the charge of Mala Roy, Councillor, Mukul Roy (Secretary of the State Committee of the Youth Congress), Nehal

Saheb and Allauddin. The Darbar was opened to public at 10 a.m. everyday and letters were received. These letters would be handed over to me, I used to read every letter and send them to Sekhar with my instructions through Manik and Kajalda. The next day all the letters would be ready for my signature.

To ensure smooth and efficient functioning of the Darbar I had divided the work:

1) would personally handle the matters connected with the Central Government.

2) Complaints about negligence of the State Govern ment and other matters connected with the State Government would be handled by Sudip Bandopadhyay, MLA.

3) Issues related to Trade Unions would be handled by Saugata Roy and Sovandeb Chattopadhyay (MLAs).

4) Legal matters (forcible occupation of land, torture, murders etc), would be sent to the Legal Cell of the State Youth Congress (advocates Kalyan Banerjee, Soumitra Pal, Asish Guha, Radha Kanta Mukherjee and others) for free legal aid. This Cell functions at my residential office. In 99% of the cases the replies have been sent directly to the persons who had written the letter, and that too when the dharna was on. The remaining few could not be answered because of non-availability of addresses. I beg forgiveness for not being able to answer these few cases amongst the thousands of letters that were handdled.

There were many who had thought that it would be impossible to tackle the voluminous correspondence. Actually, "where there is a will, there is a way"-this is something that I have learnt from experience. I do not possess the arrogance to say that I will be able to solve all problems but we can light the lamp of hope in the people if we try hard enough. Solutions can be found without the Government machinery also. The average persons have bitter experiences because the State Government does not even acknowledge their letters. Inspite of the Government machinery all matters get stuck in red tapism. However, much can be achieved if there is determination and dedication. This has been proved by the Janatar Darbar. The persons who received the letters from 10 am till 7 pm would prepare district-wise files with all sincerity and submit these to me thrice a day. As a result, it was sincerity (and not negligence) which brought success to our people's Darbar.

Even today, there are retired teachers who are starving or are half-fed because their pensions have not been released. The salary of a Home Guard is only Rs. 600/- per month. On the top of this, they have to face retrenchment within 20-25 years of service. An employee of the State Government Community Health Centre earns Rs. 50/- per month-can one imagine such a thing? One youth received his results (Mark Sheet) nine years after he passed the B.com examinations. Nine valuable years of his life has been wasted and who is responsible?

At the behest of the people I have protested against the corruption in Government, nepotism, the sad state of affairs in the education system and health services. Each issue would be raised with the back-up evidence.

By observing Intergration Day and Courtesey Day, the Darbar practically "created" milestones in human history. It will be wrong if the co-operation and affection of the local residents are not acknowledged. The Press corps used to come to our Press Corner everyday. This Darbar, having direct interaction with the people was like a trial for future plans. I recall a few small incidents. The first was like this-a girl was brought to the Dharna site at 2-30 AM from Behrampur. She had received extensive acid burns and no hospital was willing to admit her. We arranged for her admission at SSKM Hospital. The second incident relates to an youth of about 20-25 years of age. He was found sobbing at the dharna site at 6 a,m. When he was asked what was the matter, I came to know that he was employed as a Home Guard and he had received news from his village that all his household members had been shot. The name of the village was Mathurapur-Sankarpur. He did not know the whereabouts of his wife and other family members. Immediately, I requested one of the police officers on duty at the dharna site to look into the matter; he escorted the youth to Lalbazar (Police HQ of Calcutta) and made enquiries. Thirdly many ladies of ordinary family background used to visit me at nightfall. Fourthly-children (who are always dear to me) used to come and meet me during the course of the day. The fifth incident-one day a boy of 18-19 years was crying while touching my feet. I tried to figure out what was the matter. The boy sobbed and said that he had brought his own meal for me because I was not taking any food except tea throughout the day. Can such love be reciprocated?

One day I saw that a first rank-holder of Ram Krishna Mission School (Rahara) had come to meet me because he had dreamt of me the previous night.

Our dharna platform became a sanctuary of people's blessijgs and love during those 21 days. I had not realised how time had flown by. I had not slept even for a single night and not touched a grain of rice during the 21 days. Bathing was the biggest problem that I faced. The NTC office was right across the road and the employees co-operated with sincerity. I used to use their bathroom before six in the morning for my bath and after the day's work was over I would go over to change into fresh cloths.

I will always remember a street-dog. The dog won over my heart. This is not a fairy-tale; it really happened. There are many witnesses. The dog used to keep watch over me amidst all the happenings. Initially, I had not realised it. One day when I had gone over to the NTC office, for my bath, I saw the dog sitting by the bathroom. There was a public toilet-centre behind our dharna platform, but the less said about the place the better. It is advisable to inhale some extra oxygen and then go there! Whenever we went there at night, the dog would lead the way. In case anybody was inside, the dog would start barking and turn him out and then give us the green signal to go inside.

He would not allow anybody to come near me till my return to the dharna platform, and immediately after that he would clamly go off to sleep near the platform steps. One night I was suffering from intense backache and I asked someone to bring hot water. As soon as he reached the platform wit the hot water the dog started howling. Actually, the dog had came to know my constant companions, and he would not allow any other person in my immediate vicinity after night-fall. It was as though he had taken up the entire responsibility of my safety on his own shoulders.

The dog used to lie down next to our platform at the start of the day. I saw him last at about 10 p.m. on the concluding day of th Dharna. At midnight, when I was leaving the spot. I hunted high and low, but he was not to be found. Even now I wish to keep him with me in case I can find him out.

The Janatar Darbar meant endless new faces everyday, free expressions of thoughts which had been dormant so far, the unhindered, pulsating life-stream; it was like some splendid and divine ceremony of humanity. In the midst of all this were some very moving gestures-like a lady bringing a packet of biscuits for me to eat, or some pilgrims bringing sweets and flowers offerings to the deity they had gone to pray to, before coming to the dharna site.

My coleagues, who had stayed by my side from the first day till the last day of the dharna, have a special quality. They would not eat until I had some food. They used to eat only once a day, around midnight. Once in a while someone would bring food from home. I observed that many persons were bringing home-made tea, for me. They refused to listen to me when I told them not to take the trouble of bringing the tea. I felt that unless I drank a cup of 'chacha's' tea every morning the day would not go off well. Sudipda's wife Nayana, brought food for my colleagues one night. Inspite of being ill, she had cooked it herself. It was the sincere gestures of this sort which made our Janata Durbar a symbol of love, affection and sincerity. We had even developed rapport with the administrative personnel who were on duty at our dharna. During these 21 days it never occurred to me to think of who was our own and who was not. It was like a pilgrimage where everyone could meet and be together.

I am indebted to the news media. The Press Corps would come to the press corner of the dharna platform everyday at 3.30 p.m. They gave special importance to our uncompromising fight for safeguarding of human rights. Some did it by means of discussions and some others by their constructive criticism. The presence of the reporters of Ganasakti (mouthpiece of the CP(I)M should be mentioned. There had been a time when they had also said what was now being told at the dharna. Now, they may write anything against us because of their internal policy, but I do thank them for coming.

Certain persons had commented that we had diverted from the main goal of the dharna and retracted from what we had said earlier. Is this correct? Each person will judge a situation according to their attitude but we have never retracted from our main demand. We organised the programme according to the people's wishes. Nowadays, we don't hear of "people's mandate" except during election time, then also, the system of "scientific rigging" does not permit the people's mandate to be truly reflected in the ballot boxes.

Pranab Mukherjee, the then Minister of External Affairs took the initiative and spoke to the Prime Minister. He wrote a long letter informing us that our just demands would be considered with due respect. Alongside was his request for lifting the dharna. I have never shown disrespect to Pranabda and it is our duty to obey him, but the programme for 20th November was already chalked out. So I tried to contact him since the morning on that day, but I could not locate him. In the end I rang up the Prime Minister and told him how sincerely grateful I was to Pranabda. The Hon'ble Prime Minister then told me to send all details to him. He would give his views within 2-3 days.

The public gathering on 20th November has made a place for itself in history. It was a mammoth gathering.

I remembered those words.

"The flood of humanity had displaced the coward & the wrong. Pour the indomitable life, give everything you have and save your Motherland who is in danger".

I read out Pranabda's letter at the meeting and asked the assembled mass what their opinion was regarding lifting of the dharna. I was really amazed to see their uncompromising attitude. Instead of raised hands indicating their aasent, the protest resounded as the people gave their mandate against lifting of the dharna, Acutally, people roar back like this against arrogant strong-handedness of the rulers when torture and despotism reaches a certain limit. The people gave their clear message- "Carry on with the dharna, we are with you."

Just as I have many friends, there is no dearth of unseen and hidden enemies. There was every likelihood of the latter misinfoming Pranabda but can the people's durbar be worthwhile if the people's mandate does not receive due recognition? So I took a decision-the dharna would continue. I would talk to Pranabda on his return from abroad and then decide on the next step.

Certain police officers (special branch) used to report about our dharna in a disparaging way to the administration. These self-seeking persons were keeping their "king' happy. They used to continuously relay information over the walkie-talkies. It was as though they were covering a match in the play grounds and the information they would pass on was invariably wrong.

I am giving a few examples:

First report	Mamata Banerjee is ill-the dharna will not last beyond two days.
Second report	Everybody has given up hope-the dharna cannot be continued be yond seven days.
Third report	A cyclone (speed 120 kmph) is approaching. The dharna platform may be blown away. Hence they are scared and will not take any more risks.

Such police officers had only one aim-to ensure that

their king's afternoon siesta was not disturbed and to pick up whatever appreciation was thrown at them.

The DYF's (Democratic Youth Federation), conference was held on 18th November. Delegates had arrived in Calcutta from many States of India. They were under the impression that there was a "very progressive" leftist government in Bengal for the last 18 years. What they did now know was how, in this same state, (where the word revolution is deitifed), a silent revolution which had emerged from a mass satyagraha was gaining countrywide approbation.

Many red flag-bearer friends came to us that day and ovserved everything. For example, delegates from Kerala made a courtesy call at the dharna-site. Precisely at tht time, a famous journalist from Andhra Pradesh, Mr. Raju, was interviewing me. A journalist from the newspaper 'Pratideen' (Kunal Ghosh) was also present. The DYFI delegates from Kerala came to the dharna manch (platform) and spoke to us in front of everybody, including the two journalists. Why try and fish for some hidden meaning behind this? Was it because the mask of progressiveness of the left front government had been removed and the truth revealed? In democracy there will be clash of ideologies but that does not mean that good manners will be lacking. Has courtesy been defined in Karl Marx's Das Kapital? If it is there then what is the meaning given to it? I thank the delegates from Kerala, who had risen above political beliefs and ideals and had visited us.

Because of the DYF conference on 18th November, we had decided that instead of holding any meetings from the dharna manch on that day, we would observe it as Courtesy Day. Even the loudspeakers were not used, but we saw that the 'brave' members of the state unit of DYF were not prepared to show the least bit of respect towards an opposition party. I was sitting on the manch with my women co-workers. There were policemen scattered here and there. The DYF procession was passing. The so-called democratic members tore down our flags and trod on them! Targetting me and my women co-workers they started making obscene gestures, which goes against any from of decency. If the person from the administration (who was in charge in front of the manch) had not been alert, then the possibility of a mishap taking place could not be ruled out. Even after this incident, our whole-hearted welcome to the delegates from Kerala (invitees of the state unit of DYF) shows that, though other could be vile, but that should not stop us from showing courteous behaviour.

The administration learnt from the special branch report that the dharna would be lifted on 20th November. This report was proved wrong. Since the time I had received head injuries I do not get much sleep during the night. It was either 21st or 22nd November midnight, unable to sleep, I was pacing in front of the manch. Seeing me, a police officer came up and asked "Madam, are you feeling alright?" I questioned back "Why?" I was laughing to myself-they were wanting me to fall sick, so that the dharna would get lifted. What they did not know is that they may have caused injuries to me all over the body, but they have not been able to break my spine nor my mental strength, nor will they be able to do so. This is because I believe in "strength is the medicine."

At the Janatar durbar we took up issues, one after anothr, and asked the State Government for solutions. Inevitably, the adamant State Government did not give a single satisfactory reply. They said "we do not accept challenges." Actually, it is only those who have the ability to accept challenges can do so. Therefore, everyday our 'action' would be to throw challenges backed by data and facts to the State Government and their "reaction" was "not accepting them."

In this way the Janatar Durbar continued. The daily public meetings would commence at 4 p.m. and different issues would be taken up. The Speakers discussed in detail the various issues. From morning till night the people would wait eagerly. On 24th November, the Minister of State, Sree Bhubanesh Chaturvedi of the Prime Minister's office rang up and said that the Prime Minister was very sympathetic towards our struggle and he had asked the Home Minister to prepare a detailed report on lock-up and custodial deaths that had occurred in all the states and would take necessary action after discussions based on this report.

I told Bhuvaneshji that when the Prime Minister had himself assured that this state level issues would be decided on a national level, it was an acceptable proposition and deserved due respect. Since the issue was being taken up at the people's durbar, I requested him to fax the contents of Prime Minister's message, so that I could read it out to the people. Also, we did not want the critics to say that it was a ploy to lift the dharna. We were on the 20th day of the dharna and if necessary could go on for a long period. For this we were prepared mentally. The moot point was that we wanted our just demands to be given due respect.

We received the faxed copy of the Prime Minister's promise. However, the people's verdict was to decide what our next step would be. On 25th November we observed the "Black Day" of Bengal's parliamentary democracy. The slogan was:

"JYOTIBABU'S ARROGANCE FIE TO IT, FIE TO IT".

This is the same Jyoti Basu, Chief Minister of the State, who had not found it necessary, even for courtesy's sake, to send somebody to us (an opposition party) for talks.

26th November: Just like the other days, thousands of people gathered. This was without any preparation or effort on our part. Of this, our workers numbered eighty to ninty. Pankajda, Saugatada, Sovanda, Sudipda spoke. When my turn came, I showed the people the written assurance from the Prime Minister's end, which in official language is called "commitment of assurance". I told them, though the state government had remained mute, the Prime Minister had responded by giving the assurance that our demand would be taken up at the national level. This was our biggest achievement. In this context I asked the people to decide what path we should take. People in favour of lifting the dharna were to lift their hands.

The spontaneous raising of hands showed that the people's verdict was in favour of lifting the dharna. Then I said that if there was anybody who wanted the dharna to continue, he should raise his hand. I found that all the people present, with deference to the Prime Minister's assurances, wanted the dharna to be lifted. I accepted the people's mandate and after expressing my personal respect for the Prime Minister and gratitude, I lifted the dharna. The twenty one days satyagraha ended at the midnight of 26th November.

This writing will be incomplete unless the people are enlightened about certain facts that emerged from the conclusion of the dharna for protection of human rights.

Firstly, when the 19th century saw the advent of a new dimension to human philosophy in India and all over the world, Bengal was the nerve centre of this phenomenon.

The 21 days long dharna, the PM's assurances on the people's relentless struggle for the protection of human rights in Bengal had brought Bengal to the leading ranks in the struggle for human rights. Of course this came about inspite of the overall futility of the State Government.

Secondly, violation of human rights was to be judicially tried not only in Bengal but in other states of India. Without exception, all states had to abide by this.

Thirdly, the torture on arrested persons in police custody would definitely go down.

Fourthly, some form of financial assistance would be provided to the helpless family members of the persons who died in police custody.

Fifthly, the role of impartial policemen would definitely gain more importance.

Sixthly, the inclination to lay down ones' total obedience at the sacrifical post of a particular party would decrease amongst policemen. There would be more hope of getting justice and fairness from the police force.

Seventhly, people would be more organised in carrying on peaceful movements, not only against troture in police custody, but any other type of torture or wrong. Such organised protests would give a new dimension to the "People's movements'.

Most important, this 21 days of dharna had definitely been the cause of unmasking the so-called progressive left front government. The dharna has been able to enlighten the people about the hypocrisy of the left front government. On the one hand this government mouths "highly knowledgeable' speeches on human rights, organises meetings and processions but on the other hand it tramples down the people by using their party cadres or by misusing the services of certain policemen to whom they offer the lure of promotions.

The shattered heart dreams
of a new world
The shadows of dreams
one by one vanish.

Matters relating to people who have been victims of torture not only during the 18 years of CP(I)M rule but also during 1972-77 should be judged from a humanatarian angle. Regarding this, there should be no scope for procrastination, no narrow political boundaries. Only justice is needed.

Numerous letters were deposited at the Janatar Durbar. I am reproducing some of them:

The First Letter

Respected Mamatadi,

On 7.9.86 at 5 p.m. my husband was arrested by Kashipur P.S. At that time I was at home. When my father-in-law went to the police station to find out the charges for which my husband had been arrested he was not given any definite answer, and was told that my husband would be produced in the court the next morning. However, the next day (8.9.86) they did not produce my husband in the court. Seeing this my father-in-law went back to Kashipur Police Station. He was informed that my husband would be released from the police station. They did not do this. The following day, my husband was found lying unconscious in front of the police station. At that time I was unable to do anything about it. Having a small son and daughter to look after, I was unable to do anything about it at that time. Kashipur PS arrested my husband on 7.9.86, did not produce him in Court on 8.9.86 and kept him lying outside the lock up on 9.9.86.

Letter written by Smt. Rekha Guha

69, Nabin Chandra Das Road, Calcutta-40

A cutting of the report that appeared in AAJKAAL (newspaper) was enclosed. With two minor children to bring up, the lady wanted to know what she should do under these circumstances. Regarding this, does the State Government not have any moral duty?

The Second Letter

Respected Mamatadi,

At the onset, I express my regards for you. I am an unemployed youth. I am making a request to you. I had appeared for the B.com. Examinations in 1986 form Bon Hooghly college of Commerce (Calcutta-35). I failed by 8 marks. After 9-1/2 long years the college wrote to inform me that I had passed in the examination and I was asked to collect my marksheet. I went to the college and exchanged my "failed' marksheet with the "passed' marksheet. I have lost valuable years in my life because of a lapse on the part of the University or College. I have written about this in my letter to the Minister for Higher Education, and I have requested him to give me the opportunity of getting a State Government job on sympathetic grounds.

Letter written by: Sandip Basu

4, Sree Pally, D. P. Nagar, Belgharia, Calcutta-56

Sandip had made a similar request to me. My question is-who will compensate the youth for the loss of those valuable 9-1/2 years in his life? Can the State Government shirk it's responsibility? Though the Janatar Durbar (of the dharna) has closed down, the Head of our Lawyer's Cell, Kalyan Banerjee has filed an appeal in the High Court. He hopes to get justice done for Sandip. We hope for JUSTICE, JUSTICE.

The Third Letter

Respected Didi,

I humbly submit you the following facts. My husband Bisweswar Balida, S/o Sushil Balida, residing under the jurisdiction of Bhowanipur PS, Sutahati, was arrested by the police officer of Haldia PS. He was severely beaten up and sent to SDJM, Tamluk, in a that sick condition on 13.8.94.

On 10.8.94, my husband was picked up from my father's house by the officer-in-charge of Haldia PS and other police officers. When I asked them why my husband was being taken away, they abused me and threatened-"we will wipe off the sindoor (vermillion mark) from your forehead, break your sankha (a bangle that married women wear) and make you a widow'.

They badly assaulted my husband. On 12.8.94 night, police officers from Sutahati P.S. went to my father's house, broke open the lock and entered the house. Pointing a pistol at my father's head, they destroyed everything in the room, and even took away some of the moveable objects.

On 12.8.94, Friday, when I went to the P.S. to enquire about my husband I was detained there. In front of me, they beat up my husband with wooden hammers and kicked him with their boots on, in the chest, back and knees. They used other methods also to torture him. Banerjeebabu, officer of Haldia P.S. forced me to take off my ring and a pair of gold earrings. The next day, Saturday, the Haldia P.S. Officer sent my husband, in a half-dead condition, to Tamluk Court. My husband expired in 18.8.94, Sunday, at Tamluk Hospital.

I had first gone to the Court in search of my husband. Only on contacting the hospital I came to know that arrangements were being made to send my husband to Calcutta. Nobody had informed me of this. I was not allowed to see the dead body of my husband. The policemen had killed my husband through their merciless torture. I have informed many persons about the above incident. I had informed the respected Addl. S.P., Tamluk and C.I.D. West Bengal, Bhowani Bhavan, Alipur, Calcutta, but till this day no investigation has taken place.

Written by: Smt. Rekha Balida
Vill. Debhag, P.O. Debhag
P.S. Sutahati, Midanpur

Fourth Letter

Respected Didi,

I, the undersigned, am a retrenched worker from Chandan Basu's (Chief Minister's son) Durgapur Biscuit Factory. Everyone knows of the factory's closure. I come from a family of agricultural labourers. We are very poor and do not get enough to eat. There are no other earning member in the family. For refund of one's provident fund one has to go to Chandan Basu's office at Bondel Road, Calcutta. We do not have the funds to go there, nor do we know our way about in Calcutta.

Though the Durgapur factory is closed, the securitymen are still occupying the office there. Inspite of having staff posted there, why are we being made to go to Calcutta for the refund, when the job can be done in Durgapur?

We feel that if Chandan Basu had any sense, the refund forms could have been signed at the factory, the place where we had been working instead of at Calcutta. Since there is nobody else to hear us out, we are informing you. We do not have the money to go to Calcutta. We would be benefitted if the forms could be signed at Durgapur.

Respectfully,

Nepal Bauri (thumb impression)

S/o Satu Bauri

Vill. Doobjuria, P.O. Andalgram

P.S. Durgapur, Dist. Burdwan

After receiving this letter, I, personally sent one of my co-workers to help him get his dues without facing any dificulty.

We had received innumerable important letters at the Janatar Darbar. These were replied to immediately-this I have mentioned before. All the letters have been carefully filed in my office.

I was moved when the widow of Sibu Nandi (of Arambagh, Sub-division Goghat, Khanakul) who had died 13 years ago in police lock-up, came to the dharna site and added his name to the list of 298 lock-up deaths. His name was eighteenth in the list.

We have sent the list of 298 lock-up deaths to the State and Central Governments. Our demand was crystal-clear. Either a job for a member of each of the victim's family, or family-wise, a monthly pension of Rupees Fifteen Hundred.

We had been able to draw the attention of the Parliament to our just demands. Now we await the Governments' action. And if we do not get justice? The people will only decide our future course of action.

"The fog is clearing, it will clear either today or tomorrow,

Unwanted slander will be washed away,

Lives will be given up in the enemy's hands,

Till freedom blossoms and emerges from this clash,

History! There is no craving for immortality,

The present protest is placed for this moment, for the time we leave it at that."

Our so-called friends (enemies?) will definitely be happy to know that, I have been able to make the Parliamentary Standing Committee to accept our demand for a job for a member of each victim's family or a monthly pension of Rupees Fifteen Hundred per family.

At my entreaty, the respected Speaker has, in the Lok Sabha, requested the Government to take action in this matter. This victory is Human Rights' triumph.

"Our journey has started,

O Guiding Spirit,

We pay our respects to you".

4

TADA

I have been in active politics from 1970-twenty-seven years have passed by. As a student, when Congress was in power from 1972 to 1977, I had not gone to Writers' Buildings even once. Neither did I have the ability to understand what power actually meant, nor did I try to do so. At that time I would go to some leaders to ask for some help or just to show my face. The walls of my college were my boundary, and I never thought of anything beyond this.

Since the time I have entered politics I have gone through many struggles and I have been hurt over and over again. Just as I have been injured by the members of the Left Front Party, I have been subjected to one blow after another from within my own party. After Rajiv Gandhi's death I have been able to perceive one thing very well. It is not as if I have not received respect from my party, but I have also been subjected to immense indifference. I have been censured, deprived and humiliated-I have gone through turmoil, but I have never showed this.

I have suffered all the humiliation by just looking at my fellow workers and the people. At times I have protested aloud, sometimes within myself. Without understanding the trickiness of politics I have slogged like a beast of burden, soon so many of my workers shed blood. What is the value of this sacrifice today?

The traditional news media always maintains an unbiased stance. However, now-a-days some blackmarketeers, the lowest worms of the society, have started their own newspapers to establish themselves socially. If I accept their dictates, then all is well, otherwise there is poisonous character assasination in their newspapers. They secretly keep in touch with political leaders. In rotation they confer with the top leaders of CP(I)M, BJP and Congress Party. Some receive monthly retainership from these leaders. I have been sent feelers also, but have rejected these with contempt. Many of these evade income tax and excise duty. They go abroad at least once a week; selected customs officials are tipped off not to check their baggage. They are involved in many underhand deals. These persons are so well established in society that the general public never get to know of all this. They sometimes organise Receptions for ministers, donate to the Prime Minister's Relief Fund and Chief Minister's Relief Fund. To become Presidents of Puja Committees they give Rs. 1 lakh to Rs. 10 lakhs as donations. To the public they present themselves as symbols of benevolence giving speeches at public functions, all spruced up and concern showing in their eyes-trying to prove that they care for the people. The actual game is to turn black money into white. Their faults and misdeeds are overlooked, nobody speaks against them and nothing comes out against them. The only reason being that many extremely influential people have sold their souls to them!

Over anonymous phone calls, they make abominable remarks, obsequiously obeying some leader's bidding. They ring up at two in the night and threaten “”MURDER”, “”I WILL MURDER YOU” (in Hindi cinema style). They get the criminals they control to spread slander about me, so that people misunderstand me and I have to move out of the scene. They make blue prints to kill me-their battlelines encircling me (like Abhimanyu). Actually, they are very foolish, they try to chop off the branch they are sitting on. They have no value, they are like the pits of hell and are unable to differentiate between good and bad.

Can the people of Bengal reject the continuous struggles, the sacrifice of blood? All these sacrifice and forbearance are for nothing? One section of people will go on plundering and the others will be always deprived-can this be tolerated? Whatever may be the slander that they spread about me, I will see it to the end. I do not bother whether I live or die; I will continue my struggle and for the people's sake I will not move a hairline from my decision. If anybody thinks I am being too resolute, let it be so. If one thinks this is too impassioned, be it so.

The true extortioners of money and people sometimes stay in Delhi, Bombay or in Calcutta. In the dark hours of the night, they go to some nearby country house, and with some very influential political persons they drink and make merry. They gratify their self interests at the cost of the coming generation. Who will expose this to the people? Who will bell the cat? I know the job is difficult, but somebody has to do it. Even after knowing everything, some keep quiet, but I am willing to expose everything, even by betting my life on it.

As long as these masked opportunists do not stop being self-seeking, and come forward for improvement of the political and social structure, the erosion of political and social values will continue. The new generation will have to cross many a "formidable mountains, inaccessiable deep forests and deserts, invincible oceans" (adaption of Kaji Nazrul Islam's song). With firmness they have to go ahead, saying 'Bengal's soil is unconquerable-let the arrogant understand this" and say aloud spiritedly.

Let there be obstacles and impediments
We will not be defeated
We will stand up aginst injustice
Resolute we will be, not giving in a inch".

We will have to repeat the words of Rabindra Nath Tagore:

This is my prayer to thee my Lord-
Strike, Strike at the root of penury
in my heart
Give me the strength lightly to bear
My joys and sorrows
Give me the strength to make my
Love fruitful in service
Give me the strength never to
Disown the poor or bend my knees
Before insolent might
Give me strength
To raise my mind high above daily trifles
And give me the strength to
Surrender my strength to thy will with love."

I remember when I was actively involved with the TADA issue, the MPs from Bihar were forever stalling the proceedings of the Lok Sabha over holding of the Bihar Assembly elections. There was no opportunity to discuss any important matters. All over the country there were collective protests against the injustice meted under TADA. Many members of the ruling party found TADA unacceptable, but did not have the courage to openly admit it. The TADA was valid till 23.5.95. It was the right time to speak against extension of the TADA beyond this time, in the Parliament. On the other side, there were some opposition members who preferred to ignore people's problems, and by various means stalled the proceedings regularly. After considering all the aspects, I made a small placard to carry to the Parliament, though I knew this was not permissible. Since I was not getting the chance to speak, this was the only alternative. Written on the placard were the words "TA-TA TO TADA".

As a consequence, the Speaker called me to his chamber. Then I remembered a certain incident. Once Gitadi (Gita Mukherjee, MP) and I had gone to the Speaker's chamber. We had wanted to raise the issue of torture on women during Zero Hour. The Speaker had said that he did not want any MP to visit him in his chamber, regarding any matters relating to Zero Hour. Both of us were very surprised. After this incident, for over an year, I had not gone to the Speaker's chamber regarding anything. Naturally after being called by the Speaker, I felt my position of respect had been restored.

Entering the Speaker's chamber I found the Parliamentary Affairs Minister, V. C. Shukla sitting there. The Speaker started with, "Mamtaji..." for courtesy's sake I will not repeat what he said. It would not be also correct. I thanked the respected Speaker and said, "Sir, don't you know that the message has already gone to the International Press, because the National Human Rights Commission has sent letters to each MP and this Commission was set up not by the International Forum but by the Govt. of India? So, when the National Human Rights Commission has said that until and unless this Draconian Law (TADA) is withdrawn, they are not able to take up the human cause.

So how can we suppress the truth?" I love my party more than many others do. Whatever I do, it is for the good of the party. The Congress party is mass-based. Therefore, I do not agree that it is wrong to speak about the people's problems.

During Rajivji's tenure as Prime Minister I had demanded the Home Minister's resignation, sat in a 'dharna' in front of the Industries Minister's chamber, questioned the then Finance Minister on price-rise-an issue that not even the most influential leaders have had the boldness to raise. It had raised a storm in the Parliament. Then even, Rajivji had not called me once to tick me off. The then Prime Minister, Narasimha Rao, also, had not asked me why I was raising questions on the TADA issue.

It was for just reasons that I had protested against the continuation of TADA. The Prime Minister had stated in Parliament that there would be no extension of the TADA and that there had been misuse of it; but the very next day the Home Minister made the statement that it would continue. Which was correct? If there was confusion within one's own walls, then naturally, the general public would want to know the correct facts.

At this time, when I was being very voluble regarding th misuse of the TADA, the opportunists spread slander about me, smearing my name with distorted facts. I am informing those opportunists that the Chairperson of the National Human Rights Commissions had sent me a letter (No: 16/1/CH/NHRC-95) which was received by me on 20th February, 1995. Fearing that my version of the letter may lead to exaggeration, I am reproducing the letter:

No: (1) Human Rights have been defined in section 2(d) of the Act and mean the rights relating to life, liberty, equality and dignity of the individual guaranteed by the constitution as embodied in the International

Covenants and enforceable by courts of India. Section 12 of the Act enumerates the function of the Commission. Sub-section (d) requires the Commission to review the safeguards provided by or under the Constitution or any law for the time being in force for the protection of human rights and recommended measures for their effective implementation. Sub-section (f) requires the Commission to study treaties and other instruments on human rights and make recommendation for their effective implementation.

No: (2) In 1984, when terrorist activities increased in Punjab, the Terrorist Affected Area (Special Courts) Act 1984 was legislated. As terrorist activities increased and functioning of the special courts became difficult Parliament legislated the Terrorist and Disruptive Activities (Prevention) Act, 28, of 1987. This law was a temporary legislation mainly intended to deal with the prevailing situation in Punjab. It made considerable deviations from the normal to meet the emergent situation. The principal ones are:

a) Raising the presumption of guilt and shifting the burden on the accused to establish his innocence.

b) Drawing the presumption of guilt for possession of certain unauthorised arms in special areas.

c) Making confession before a police officer admissible in evidence.

d) Providing protection to witness such as keeping their identity and address secret and requiring avoidence of the mention of their names and address in orders of judgement or in any records of the case accessible to the public

e) Modifying the provisions of the Code of Criminal Procedure particularly in regard to the time for investigation and grant of bail. The title of the Act indicates that it was intended to combat terrorist activities and was not, therefore, intended to apply to areas where such activities were not visible.

The Act has, however been extended to the whole country and had been freely applied to situation not contemplated by the Act.

No:(3)The Constitution assured the dignity of the individual. The fundamental rights guaranteed life in every facet of it.

Besides the above, in 1984, India had been a participating nation at the Universal Declaration for Human Rights.

Watch out, opportunists-now I am going to reproduce the relevant portion of the letter from National Human Rights Commission:

No: 3 The Indian Evidence Act, 1872, almost 125 years old, had provided that confession before a police officer would not be taken as evidence. Article 20(3) of the Constitution which is one of the fundamental rights of our citizens, proclaims that no person accused of any offence, shall be compelled to be a witness, against himself. Notwith standing this, the special provision in TADA makes the confession before a police officer admissible; the withholding of particulars of witness, takes away the guarantee of fair trial for accused persons. The shift of presumption makes in difficult for the TADA accused to establish his innocence to get bail and the amendment of the Code of Criminal Procedure keeps the accused in jail for a long period of six months as against the maximum limit of three months provided in Section 167(2) of the Code of Criminal Procedure. If investigation in a case of murder can be completed in 90 days and if not completed, bail is admissible to a murderer as an automatic process, there can be no justification for a longer period to be provided in respect of TADA matter.

The National Human Rights Commission has further opined:

No: (4)The TADA Legislation is, indeed, draconian in pl/ 14effect and character and has been looked down upon as incompatible with our cultural traditions, legal history and treaty obligations. Provisions of the statute as such have yielded to abuse and on account of such a situation, the Act has been misused over the years and thousands of innocent people who could have been otherwise dealt with, have been roped in to languish in jail, may feel that the police have found it a convenient silence opposition and that it has been frequently abused for political consideration.

No: (5)The law and order machinery should not be permitted to operate any longer under the cover of such a Black Law.

No: (6) The Act itself has been condemned both within the country and internationally as violating our International Treaty obligations.We set liberty of the individual as our goal in the freedom struggle. How can any of our law-makers be party to a system of legalising undue curtailment there of? The Act operates unjustly and has at its very base a foundation of injustice.

Now the conclusion, which is very important; "In Indian democratic set-up, equality is the rule and the rule of law provides the umbrella under which all are treated at par in real life. I remind you that you have entrusted the

Commission with the charges of maintaining human rights and the commission is finding it difficult to do so unless this DRACONIAN LAW is removed from the statute book".

Ms. Mamata Banerjee
Member of Parliament

Sri Ranganath Misra
Chairman
National Human Rights Commission

I have one question for the opportunists who had been scared out of their wits when the TADA was being volubly opposed-now that the TADA has lapsed, are they sleeping undisturbed? Otherwise they should arrange for the required medical treatment, and even go to England and America for it, in keeping with their 'status'. There is nothing to object about that! There is one request-before selling your soul to anyone let the people know what price you are selling yourself at. Self-seekers, whatever disguise you may assume, your true self will be revealed to the people one day. Then the people will not forgive you.

The following may be a myth, but I have used it for reference. In Ramayana (which I have read) Sita had to undergo Agnipariksha (Test of Fire) to be freed from the conspiracy woven by the schemers. Though Ramayana's Ram or Ayodhya are no more, the group of schemers are still to be found, their souls as terrifying as poisonous snakes. Due to the compromises they make, their profit and loss accounts reflect only gain and no loss. They hit the headlines in newspapers. And, from amongst them, one may, by lobbying, even get the Bharat Ratna. It is a shame, but whose shame is it? Even 'shame' will turn away from them feeling disgraced. Their conscience is mortgaged to the "give and take' trade. With complete disregard for the people, all that they do is misuse the power that they have. People watch these rich and sauve counterfeits, cheats, self-interest seekers and think where is the end?

I deem it necessary to write down and place before the

people the reasons behind my letter of resignation, dt. 24.5.95 to the Hon'ble Speker. I was facing a dilemma over an important comment made by the Hon'ble Speaker. Exactly what had I tried to say that day? I had merely asked what was the Government's decision regarding the TADA detainees (about 5000 persons) since the Act had lapsed. Clause 2 of the TADA stated that in case the Act lapsed, the detainees under the Act would be tried under the lapsed Act. What would happen to the innocent people who were in no way terrorists but were victims of the misuse of TADA by their respective State Governments?

The Hon'ble Speaker had told me on that day that: (1) as a member of the treasury bench I could not raise this issue. (2) He did not approve of my dharna at the feet of the statue of Gandhiji within the grounds of Parliament House.

I had repeatedly tried to point out to the Speaker that if he made comments in the House, the same would be taken as a 'ruling'. Such comments would therefore, throttle the voice of the participants of any democratic movement. If a peaceful dharna is staged at the feet of the Father of the Nation, Mahatma Gandhi, the symbol of secularism and the highest priest of Ahimsa, then any such act of silent protest against wrong gets elevated to the nobel status of a satygraha. In case the Parliament has any reservations about such actions, then the very voice of protest will one day fall silent and the future of democracy will be thrown to dust.

The wanton ruling class will repeatedly damage the foundations of democracy. People will lose their right to protest. If the democracy's highest court (or the Indian Parliament) holds the people's voice of protest as a captive in the dark prisons, the people's fundamental rights, democratic rights and human rights will truly be mortified and aggrieved.

It is true that I was a member of the ruling party, but what about my conscience? That was not mortgaged to any party. The efforts of my Party colleagues for my election deserves to be acknowledged, but what is more important to me are the people who elected me as a Member of Parliament.

Swami Vivekananda had said "I never heard a cow tell a lie, but it is only a cow, never a man". Since the cow does not possess the power of speech, so where is the opportunity for her to tell a lie? When we do possess the power of speech, are we not duty-bound to show a minimum protest? That is why, on that day (i.e. 24.5.95) I had to make a choice and decided as to which was more important-the designation of a Member of Parliament or Human Rights? My conscience found the answer in the spontaneity of my emotions; no designation or position lasts forever. There is only one factor which is permanent in a democracy and that is the people.

So I made no delay in deciding that I would not tolerate this damaging insult to democracy. The people of Bengal would not have forgiven me if I had compromised and said "YES SIR" for the sake of my 'stamp'. How would I bear the burden of this shame? In the depths of my soul those immortal words of Rabindra Nath Tagore resounded: "Where the mind is without fear and the head is held high".

The innermost voice of those neglected people seemed to strike my conscience through the words of Rabindra Nath Tagore. From within my mind someone seemed to be singing "Give me the strength never to disown the poor or to bend my knes before insolent might". I did something which had never happened before in the history of Parliament-I stood inside the House, handed over my letter of resignation while the House was in session and came out.

Some may approve of this decision of mine; some may disapprove. Some may come to their own conclusions to please somebody else or may go for alliances for the sake of electoral gains. At the same time one must remember that the speaker's position should be strictly impartial and dignified. It is like an amulet for safeguarding the law and democratic rights. The person who holds this position may have personal views, but it should never be at the cost of mortgaging the conscience at the gallows. On that day I had taken the decision that only the people would have the final say on the matter (i.e. the reason for my resignation).

It is the people who can pave the way in; at the same time they can pave the way out also. It is our duty to safeguard the honour of the people. Although many may still be curious and have questions to ask, it must be made clear that I had handed over my resignation to the Speaker for one and only reason-to protest against wrong.

My well-wishers (do they really wish for my well being?) have on many occasions said that I have resigned too often. I had resigned from the cabinet because I wanted to devote more time to Bengal. Only a person who lives in a fool's paradise can go on believing that I will let myself be insulted because I have raised the issue of democratic rights or that I will continue as a Member just to be able to offer "puja" to a certain "deity" while democratic and moral values are made irrelevant and powerless. I am willing to risk my life to do whatever is necessary to ensure that Bengal's honour is in no way hurt. The people of Bengal can repose their faith in me over this matter without any fear. It is this trust that I have over the people which is my support for the future. I will not allow my Motherland's honour to be laid to the dust. The soil of Bengal, the water of Bengal are our invaluable assets. Bengal is still our pride and our hope. It was Bengal who had in the past lit up the beacon in the spheres of civilisation, culture, creativity etc. Bengal's valour and bravery had no parallel. When I think of this I feel emotionally thrilled.

The people of Bengal may worry about what will happen to their problems after my resignation from Parliament. I have not gone to Parliament for six months since I handed over my resignation to the Speaker on 24.5.95. As a result, perhaps my annual quota of two admissions to the Central School had been wasted; Perhaps I have not been able to allot 30 domestic gas connections and provided 10 telephone connections from my quota. Although the letter of resignation has not been accepted, I have not used my MPs letterhead on moral grounds for six months. If I had availed of the air tickets and other benefits to which a MP is entitled, I would perhaps been able to earn an additional amount of Rs. 50,000/- at least in these six months and thus enhanced my personal savings. But, I have not bowed down in this battle over moral issues.

As a rule I dont go to Delhi often. I go when there is some important work, but I never go there just to mark my attendence and to make some money in the process. If one goes on tour in connection with the various Parliamentary Committees, quite a good amount of money can be drawn on account of TA & DA. This is apart from the various other perquisites. As far as I remember, I have gone on such tours on two occasions only in the last ten years (since my election from Jadavpur Constituency in 1984). When I was a Minister of Sports, I had many opportunities for visiting China, Japan, USA and other countries. I did not go for only one reason-that was to save the money of the Ministry. While I was a Minister I had gone to the neighbouring country, Maldives. The programme was for three days-I had gone to participate in the

Meeting of Ministers of the Commonwealth. I had returned the US10100/- that the Ministry had given to me on account of entertainment allowance. Of course, this created a problem for the Ministry. They repeatedly asked me as to how they would redeposit the money. I told them to convert the foreign currency to Indian Rupee and to deposit this in the department-then the problem would be solved. The second tour was at Colombo. It was in connection with a SAARC meet. Smt. Geeta Mukherjee, Supriya Chatterjee and others were also included in the delegation. On that occassion also I did not draw any entertainment allowance from the department.

While I was standing at the Brigade Parade Ground on 25.11.92, I relinquished my Ministerial Post. By nightfall, my letter of resignation had reached the Prime Minister's Office. The resignation was accepted on 18.1.93. As I was officially a Minister during this interim period, I received the Minister's salary also, but I gave this entire sum to the National Sports Welfare Fund by account Payee Cheque. I did not accept or utilise any of the perquisites and privileges that a Minister is entitled to during this period on moral grounds.

I have received several invitations to go abroad after my resignation. I was invited to go with a team headed by the Speaker (Commonwealth Conference). I had declined, because it would mean staying away from Bengal for a long time. In my capacity as a MP, I was supposed to attened a special programme in USA, but I did not go. I have conveyed my regrets and turned down an invitation to go to Beijing. When Rajiv Gandhi was the Prime Minister however, I had to go the Russia on three occasions. I also went to Vietnam, Bangkok, Kuala Lampur, London, Paris, Angola and S. Africa as a representative of my Party.

Therefore, I have no regrets for having submitted my

resignation from Parliament. To me, it is not what post I hold that counts, but it is the willingness to work which is of utmost importance. For the last 6 months I have forwarded different cases in my capacity as the President of the State Youth Congress (explanations: cases here refers to appeals made by citizens regarding their day to day problems and harrassments that they face). The response to my letters has been good and I have received replies also. I have done the maximum possible that can be done by a person of insignificant status to satisfy the common people's wants.

Today is 3.12.95. I am writing this on my way to Delhi. The Speaker has invited me for tea at his Chamber on 4.12.95. I am going to Delhi because the invitation has been conveyed with due respect. I dont know what my next decision will be, but whatever it may be, the people will certainly come to know of it.

4.12.1995: After returning from the Speaker's chamber just now, I have decided that I will join Parliament from tomorrow. The Speaker has himself requested me to forget the "misunderstanding" and has asked me, with due respect, to attend the Lok Sabha. On a personal level, I am grateful to the Speaker. He has upheld the democratic norms by his honourable and courteous approach while asking me to attend Parliament. Apart from this, my resignation was still not accepted. So I decided to again attend Parliament. While taking this decision I had taken into consideration the following factors:

1) The Speaker could not be dishonoured.

2) The honour of Parliament had to be maintained.

3) Above all, the aspirations of the people had to be conveyed and rightly placed to the highest forum i.e. Parliament.ci

I was confident that I had not committed any wrong by tendering my resignation. I knew that the honour that was my due would be restored one day or another. Although we belong to different political parties, I had casually requested Saifuddin Chowdhury (while I was chating with him) to accompany me to the Speaker's Chamber. He had agreed immediately. He is the witness to the conversation between the Speaker and myself. My thanks to Saifuddin.

5

STRUGGLE FOR JUSTICE

Man's survival centres around the path of struggle for fulfilling one's dreams. When the sapling grows to become a gigantic tree, it has to face nature's fury. A child grows amidst tears and laughter without realizing many things; slowly his sense of realization develops and he learns what is sorrow and what is joy. Life's journey takes myriad paths-for some the passage is bright and cheerful and for other it is full of adversity. Some choose the fast track to acquire comforts and affluence; Some in their life's journey receive grief, toil, trouble and despair. Some choose the path of idealism. It is in this path where the deep-rooted faith gives birth to certain beliefs. Belief, like a small boat in turbulent waters, has to face hostile waves also. When belief knows that it shall not succumb to falsehood, then it becomes the birthplace of new 'path of life'. At the very inception of this new way of life, belief brings struggle and the compulsion to move fast amidst dangers, At times this beings the storm of obstacles. Then, some feel-"Now they are finished. Aren't they in a fix now?" And, I think-

"Really?" Isn't coming to this conclusion a bit hasty? After all the term "in a fix" has a deeper meaning. If this term is used with utter confidence and not because there exists certain apprehensions, then, do the same persons (who use this term) have the guts to answer certain questions that can be asked? Certainly there is a necessity to put this to test also.

There are many ways and means to put people in a fix. It is not that such devious strategies have not been tried. When such moves cannot defeat the countermoves, then the masks are unveiled and the bitter conspiracies are revealed.

The 1996 elections approached and the people of Bengal hoped that there would be a change in the government. Therefore there was no dearth in the enthusiasm amongst the congress workers; but alliances were made by some heavy weights of Delhi (they are also referred to as the saviours of the Marxists by their critics). Some friends of the Marxists whose roots are deeply embedded in Delhi-the Congress (Marxists) wove the web of conspiracy so that the Marxists would not be harmed in Bengal and Congress would come to power at the centre. This was done at the cost of the prospects of the Congress in Bengal.

Therefore, it has become imperative to identify and demarcate what is the mainstream and what is not the mainstream within the Congress. When a political party stoops to the level of using party designations as a means of allurement or appeasement and tries to deter the mainstream, then cannot an alternate leader with the right attitude to counter these obstacles be found? Will a helmsman who can sing the words "Break, Break down the barrieers" be found?

It is my personal belief that if there is a boat then there

shall be a helmsman and if this boat carries the people then the helmsman will reach them to the correct distination. The boat which shall carry the people-that is the bearer of democracy-shall be like the ordinary ferry that shall cater to the everyday needs of the people. It need not have adornments and embellishments. The stamps of status and symbol does not last long but the common man's 'ordinary' status is for a lifetime. Those who cannot move without their crowns for even a single moment will be tied down by a crowns beneath which lies deceit and the 'so alluring' misdeeds. There shall be a contingent of demons to guard this crown so that it never slips and falls. And, there are the so-called politicians who will give fiery speeches year after year (surpassing Rabindra Nath Tagore even!) and add spit and polish to the 'crown' they wear. These persons will neither deliver anything new nor will they create anything.

So, what is necessary is an analysis and assessment of what the common man wants. What alternate choice do they have? What is needed? The same replay of the oftenacted game of hide and seek? Or a situation where the reality is encountered face to face and mistakes are assessed, accepted and rectified and the only game that is played is 'credibility'. People will believe in the credibility only if there is the underlying sincerity. It must be remembered that people's confidence can be won only when there is a real difference between tigers and the paper tiger.

Although the people of West Bengal wanted a change from the Leftist Rule, deals were struck-with the wholehearted co-operation of the Congress the seat adjustments were decided-which seat would go to the Congress-which would go to the CP(I)M-Congress would make gains in Bengal but would not cross the 100 figure mark.

There were many things I could not come to terms

with. As a mark of protest against the inclusion of certain anti-socials in the Congress candidates' list, I had decided not to contest in 1996. After seeing the final list I had wept silently for three whole days. I could not accept such treachery. So I decided to withdraw my candidature. I stayed at a colleague's residence for three days so that no one could stop me. But I could not even reach the Returning Officer; thousands of colleagues and the people obstructed me. My car was surrounded by thousands-some had slashed their torso, some threatened to commit suicide. My car could not even move an inch and I had to ultimately turn back. It was Sudip Bandopadhyay (MLA) who had brought my symbol paper from the so-called Congress and submitted it. The congress leadership had felt ashamed of even writing my name in the 'symbol paper'. Both the Congress and the CP(I)M had publicised the fact that no one had ever won twice from my South Calcutta constituency. Inspite of the maligning and the rigging I defeated the CP(I)M and BJP. With the people's blessings, as a Congress candidate I won by the highest margin.

There was rigging at booth after booth; I remember how I had to face the guns and goons at the counting centre at 1 a.m. and protect my workers to stop the attempt to rig the counting also. I am the sole enemy of the Congress and the CP(I)M. So there were many secret meetings held at the Administrative level to ensure my defeat, but they failed because of the people's blessings and the unstinted efforts of my co-workers.

The elections were over; no Party secured majority. Even before we reached Delhi or received our certificate declaring us as winning candidates, the Congress leadership announced unconditional support to the United Front Government. I had repeatedly tried to make the ledership at Delhi understand that we ought to play the role of an effective opposition since the people had not given us the mandate to form the govenment. Nobody paid heed at that time.

Instead, Congress extended support to a government which was being "remote controlled" by the CPI(M)-the very CPI(M) against whom we had fought in the election and some Congress candidates had won.

Why had it been necessary for the Congress to flight with partners of the United Front at the time of the elections-the Telegu Desam in Andhra Pradesh, the Janata Dal in Orissa, Bihar and Uttar Pradesh, the CPI(M) in Bengal, Kerala and Tripura? So, many Congress workers had lost their lives or had to flee from their homes as a sequel to the poll-related clashes with the CPI(M). For these workers the Congress leaders did not spare a thoughts, all they were after was power. Both, Indira Gandhi and Rajiv Gandhi had been leaders of the opposition when the need arose and they had been able to rejuvenate the Congress party. They had ensured the survival of the party. Now, the totally confused Congress leadership supplied the 'life-giving' oxygen to the United Front just to save themselves from the various cases they are embroiled in.

All of a sudden, Chacha Sitaram Kesari clashed with the Deve Gowda Government and the chorus 'Remove Deve Gowda' broke out. One hundred and forty-one Members of Parliament had repeatedly asked the leadership to take into account the opinion of the MPs; at least they were to be allowed to express their views at the forum for MPs-the Congress Parliamentary Party. But the 141 MPs were treated like bonded labour and their opinion hardly mattered. They were given the party whip to vote against Deve Gowda. Although the Deve Gowda Government had misused certain "impartial organisations" for the sake of political and party considerations, it had been assertive in many aspects. It will be wrong on my part if I do not mention two incidents. When Deve Gowda had been Prime Minister I had sought appointments with him on a couple of occasions on matters concerning public welfare, and he did meet me at such short notice. I remember, while he was returning after the election campaign in Uttar Pradesh, he had directly sent word from the aircraft itself to his office that he would meet me-this was related to a problem faced by farmers. When it was no longer possible to suppress certain 'files' it became necessary to remove Deve Gowda. It was an ego clash whereby the leader was changed but the same set-up continued. Such was the 'Left-Left' politics of the leader of one hundred and forty one Congress MPs-Chacha Kesari.

Then came the 'friendly' Gujral Government remote controlled by two persons-the Leftist Harkisen Surjeet and Kesariji. Now the files could be cleared easily-but the obstruction came in the form of Jain Commission! In the midst of this, Chachaji conducted the farcical elections through his henchmen and the AICC session was held at the Netaji Indoor Stadium. Goons openly rigged the elections for the Working Committee. Votes of members who were dead or absent were utilised. Kesariji wanted to teach us a lesson because we had pointed our that the elections had been a farce in Bengal and we were the Congress mainstream. So Kesariji decided to hold the AICC session at Calcutta.

Of course, before this, we had started touring the districts to interact with the grassroot Congress workers and to get their opinion. In the meantime, we had a huge meeting as per schedule at Calcutta in the memory of the martyrs of 21st July. Through the grassroot workers were demanding an 'outdoor' meeting to give back a fitting reply to the arrogance of the AICC and it's 'Indoor' meeting, I was wondering whether a meeting on 9th August, so close to the heels of the 21st July meeting would be up to the mark.

But alongwith this I realised that such arrogance had to be given a fitting reply-the workers honour had to be upheld-even if it rained, even if there was no food or staying accomodation for the workers and even if they had to make sacrifices. For the sake of the workers honour and self-respect an 'outdoor' meeting was necessary to counter the 'indoor' meeting. They had hordes of leaders, opulence and five-star arrangements. And, we had the 'little star' workers. So the 'indoor' Congress remained closeted indoors while we, on 9th August, in the year of the 50th anniversary of the nation's independence, were able to hold our meeting. A meeting that took place on the roads of Calcutta with the statue of Gandhiji as witness and the spontaneous support of the workers-a meeting that upheld the dignity of the grass-root workers.

On that historic Martyrs' Day, the main demand of the Congress workers and the people was to teach the AICC a lesson.

So, it was the grass-root workers who formed the Trinumul (Grass-root) Congress Committee. I proposed the name of Sree Pankaj Banerjee (MLA), who had always stood by the Congress workers, as President. Sree Sudip Bandopadhyay (MLA) and Akbar Ali Khondokar (MLA) seconded this. This was placed before the assembly of the grass-root workers. They unanimously supported the proposal. After this, as a symbolic gesture, I proposed the name of Dr. Sushobhan Banerjee (a reputed physician) as the President of a District Committee. This was seconded by Sree Sovandeb Chattopadhyay (MLA), Sree Sadhan

Pandey (MLA) and Sree Sanjoy Bakshi (MLA). The grass-root workers, with the show of hands, elected him unanimously in the thoroughfare of Calcutta. An event that is unimaginable! In the game of Indoor and Outdoor, the Outdoor team won the Champion Trophy. And the grass-root workers, with the dust of the roads their only blessing and emotions raging against the so-called leaders, went back filled with dreams of freeing Bengal from the clutches of the CP(I)M.

And the message of the grass-root was spread by the grass-root workers to the booth-level.

Now, to revert to what I had started with-the Left-Left game played by Sitaram Kesari. The strategy was to remove Deve Gowda, become the supreme power, dispose the Gujral Government and then become Prime Minister. For this the trumped-up game was played-the No Confidence Motion was not to be taken up and the Jain Commission Report was not to be discussed-to elevate Sitaram Kesari to the Prime Minister's chair. His tune had changed-'Left' had become 'self'. And, over the issue of Rajiv Gandhi's assassination, it took ten days of deliberations before the much sought after Congress support was withdrawn by the Congress leadership. When the decision was taken it was done with much relunctance and without the courtesy of a general body meeting of the Congress Parliamentary Party. The destiny was decided by a group of 'highly honourable' Rajya Sabha members, some of whom had not even won Panchyat elections.

Then, suddenly a decision was taken that the Congress would form the Government and the President was informed of this. And, the 'pious' king-makers of the United Front, a Government that had existed for eighteen months on the 'life-saving' oxygen provided by the Congress, who had pillaged during this period and passed on the burden to the people in the form of taxes, suddenly found the same Congress untouchable. From the beginning we had said that the Congress should remain in the opposition because this had been the people's mandate. Inspite of being the single largest party in the 1989 elections, Rajiv Gandhi had abided by the people's mandate. He had taken up the role of the leader of the opposition and was able to revive the party. After losing the elections in 1977, Smt. Indira Gandhi, while in the opposition, was able to rejuvenate the party and bring it back to power.

And, the present day leaders put their personal interests before anything else; they are power crazy and don't spare a thought for the people and the country's welfare.

Firstly, I had tried to have the Jain Commission Report discussed in Parliament by requesting for the No Confidence Motion. I had to face tremendous pressure, so that I would withdraw the Motion.

But I was unable to accept the contradiction-on the one hand the Gujral Government would not be allowed to function as long as the DMK remained in the Cabinet and on the other hand, the No-Confidence motion was not to be discussed. I refused to withdraw the motion because I wanted to stop the trumped-up game being played by the Left-Right-Middlemen Combine.

Secondly, despite having pointed out to the leadership that the issue should be discussed with the Congress Parliamentary Party MPs, why were Yechury, Gujral and Naidu of the UF deciding how the internal affairs of the Congress party were to be conducted?-Why were they deciding what policy should be taken by the Congress? What was unforgivable was the indecision, day after day, regarding withdrawing support on the issue of the particular assassination by which the party lost it's supreme leader Rajiv Gandhi.

While the rigmarole was going on over the decision to be taken regarding the issue of Rajiv Gandhi's assassination, I had asked a person who had been a close associate of Rajivji, what would be the reaction if ordinary members like him and I were murdered, when it was taking days to come to any conclusive decision over such an important matter like Rajivji's assassination? He had replied, "They will send a wreathe but that shall be accompanied with a bill."

The bitter truth that we face today is that our fate hangs by the slender thread of political hypocrisy. Before the elections the people's mandate is sought by projection a certain combination or alliance between political parties; when the elections are over, the people's mandate and their interest are cast aside and self-interest of the leaders overtakes. Then, combinations and alliances are reversed even if this goes against the people's mandate in the scramble for grabbing power and forming the Government. Is this not deceiving the people? The election fight between the Congress and the CPI(M) took place in Bengal, Tripura and Kerala. After the elections the two parties decided to function together as friends of the United Front Government. In Uttar Pradesh, Bihar and Andhra Pradesh the election fight was between the Congress and the Janata Dal and Telegu Desham Party. The Congress workers had to sacrifice a great deal to put up a tough fight. Then 'fate' decided that they would have to accept a complete reversal of policy regarding the same party they had fought against.

Some political leaders have the misguided notion that the people of India are swayed by the talk of communalism and secularism and their votes are influenced by such concepts. Time compels me to be brief in my answer to this issue-People shall repose their faith only in that Government which looks after the welfare of the people and the unity and stability of the nation. Why should the communalism and secularism cards be allowed to be used as instruments to manoeuvre the people's mandate repeatedly? The main issue should be:

"Neither so called secularism,
Nor so called communalism,
This country can be saved
only with HUMANISM."